COOK'S COLLECTION

MEAT FREE

*Fuss-free and tasty recipe ideas
for the modern cook*

CONTENTS

INTRODUCTION

The vegetarian diet is a feast of colour, vibrancy and flavour – the recipes in this book combine the best of natural ingredients in healthy, mouthwatering meals, along with some treats! Whether you're a committed vegetarian, or a meat-eater wanting inspiration for meat-free days, veggie meals are a celebration of bold flavours and exciting textures.

Being vegetarian means enjoying a diet that is free from animal-derived products like meat and fish. Eating large quantities of meat, both fresh and processed, has been linked to disease and a range of health problems, so many of us are now adopting meat-free days each week, or going totally vegetarian.

With this shift in thinking there has never been a more exciting time to start cooking and eating veggie food! No longer solely reliant on meat substitutes and a few reliable ingredients, modern vegetarian dishes are exciting, varied and utterly delicious, made using natural, vegetarian ingredients.

For some eating meat-free is an easy and natural decision to make, while for others it takes a little bit of time to get used to the switch in thinking. Even if you don't jump straight in, making small changes and gradually reducing the amount of meat and animal-derived products you eat will help you get started and can have a positive impact on your health. Ensuring that you eat a balanced meat-free diet complete with lots of fresh vegetables, fruit, grains, pulses, beans, nuts, seeds and a little dairy is a good way to stay healthy.

This book guides you through great vegetarian ideas for every meal throughout the day, including breakfast, lunch, dinner, desserts and baking. With healthy recipes, quick meals, comfort food, special occasion ideas and a few treats, it can be used as a complete meat-free cookbook for the whole family. You can use it one day or every day during the week.

The secret to eating well on a veggie diet is freshness and quality. A well-planned meat-free diet will give you variety and all the nutrients you need. Try to source your vegetables at your local farmers' market or greengrocer; for maximum flavour and nutrients, make sure that anything you buy is crisp and shiny. If you have a garden or access to an allotment, have a go at growing your own. Apart from the huge sense of satisfaction when you pull that first carrot out of the ground, you'll know exactly what you're eating, especially if you use organic seeds and natural fertilisers.

Fruit and vegetables are the most obvious stars of a veggie diet and can be combined in a whole host of ways to make health-packed, delicious dishes any time of the day. Some of these combinations may surprise you – mix up your usual breakfast and try Crushed Edamame & Avocado Toasts (see page 28) for a delicious and filling start to the day.

Eggs, cheese, beans and pulses have long been recognised as the go-to ingredients for veggie protein. A word of warning, when you're using dried beans, be sure to soak them for at least five hours, then boil them for 10 minutes to remove any toxins. Tofu is also a great source of protein and a handy addition to stews and stir-fries.

Another must-have in the vegetarian diet is grains. Most grains are useful sources of vitamins, minerals and carbohydrates, but some are nutritional powerhouses and are perfect for anyone on a plant-based diet. Quinoa is a high-protein, mineral-dense seed that can be used whole in main dishes – try spicy Quinoa Chilli (see page 120), or ground into flour and used in baked recipes.

Buckwheat flour, ground from a seed, also has a high protein content and many health benefits, including lowering cholesterol. Black rice is another protein-rich grain. Highly versatile, it can be used both in savoury dishes and desserts.

Nuts and seeds pack a big nutritional punch for their size. They make great power snacks and are tasty additions to salads, breakfasts and desserts. They can also up the nutritional content of a recipe and add extra texture and flavour. Chia seeds are a good source of protein and minerals. Just sprinkle them over yogurt like the Greek-style Yogurt with Orange Zest & Toasted Seeds (see page 13), or use them in delicious drinks.

While it's obvious to avoid meat and fish when following a veggie diet, there are some ready-made products that contain non-vegetarian ingredients that you'll want to avoid too. Things like rennet, which is an animal-derived product, are used in the production of non-vegetarian cheeses, so make sure any cheese you buy is labelled 'vegetarian'. Non-vegetarian Worcestershire sauce contains anchovies, so look for the vegetarian version.

And don't forget sweet treats. Non-vegetarian gelatine is an animal product and appears in sweets and desserts, so check ready-made products to make sure they are vegetarian. Non-vegetarian wine is refined using animal-derived products, so ensure you buy and cook with vegetarian wine. There are excellent vegetarian alternatives available for many types of ingredients – always check the label if you're not sure about an ingredient.

The recipes in this book provide a treasure trove of delicious vegetarian dishes – so get cooking and discover how tasty and easy meat-free eating can be!

CHAPTER ONE

BREAKFAST

NUTTY GRANOLA SUNDAES
WITH YOGURT & MANGO

INGREDIENTS

100 g/3½ oz whole almonds,
  roughly chopped
75 g/2¾ oz pecan nuts, roughly
  chopped
50 g/1¾ oz cashew nuts, roughly
  chopped
50 g/1¾ oz sunflower seeds
100 g/3½ oz pumpkin seeds
2 tbsp sesame seeds
125 g/4½ oz rolled oats
3 tbsp coconut oil
3 tbsp maple syrup
2 tsp ground cinnamon
100 g/3½ oz dried cranberries
8 tbsp Greek-style natural yogurt
1 mango, stoned, peeled and
  chopped

1. Preheat the oven to 180°C/350°F/Gas Mark 4.

2. Place the nuts in a large bowl with the seeds and oats and mix well together.

3. In a small saucepan, combine the coconut oil, maple syrup and cinnamon over a medium heat. When the coconut oil has melted, remove from the heat and stir into the nut mixture, mixing well.

4. Evenly spread the mixture over a baking sheet and bake in the preheated oven for 30–35 minutes, shaking and stirring occasionally, until golden.

5. Remove from the oven and leave to cool before stirring in the cranberries.

6. Divide the granola between six bowls and serve layered with yogurt and chopped mango.

RAW CARROT, APPLE &
GOJI BIRCHER MUESLI

SERVES: *4* | **PREP:** *15 mins, plus chilling* | **COOK:** *No cooking*

INGREDIENTS

125 g/4½ oz buckwheat flakes

1 carrot, grated

2 red-skinned apples

150 ml/5 fl oz apple juice

150 ml/5 fl oz almond milk

1½ tbsp dried goji berries

2 tbsp chopped hazelnuts

2 tbsp chopped dried apricots

1½ tbsp shelled pistachio nuts

1 tbsp sunflower seeds

1. Put the buckwheat flakes and carrot in a large bowl. Core, thinly slice and chop one of the apples and add to the bowl. Stir the bowl contents well until thoroughly combined. Stir in the apple juice, almond milk and 1 tablespoon of the goji berries. Cover and leave in the refrigerator overnight.

2. Stir the hazelnuts into the bowl. Core, thinly slice and chop the remaining apple.

3. Divide the muesli between serving dishes and sprinkle the apple, remaining goji berries, apricots, pistachio nuts and sunflower seeds over the muesli. Serve immediately.

FIG & WATERMELON
SALAD

SERVES: 4 | **PREP:** 20–25 mins, plus cooling & chilling | **COOK:** 5 mins

INGREDIENTS

1.5 kg/3 lb 5 oz watermelon
115 g/4 oz seedless black grapes
4 figs

SYRUP DRESSING

1 lime
grated rind and juice of 1 orange
1 tbsp maple syrup
2 tbsp honey

1. Cut the watermelon into wedges and scoop out and discard the seeds. Cut the flesh away from the rind, then chop the flesh into 2.5-cm/1-inch cubes.

2. Put the cubes in a bowl with the grapes. Cut each fig lengthways into eight wedges and add to the bowl.

3. Grate the lime and mix the rind with the orange rind and juice, maple syrup and honey in a small saucepan. Bring to the boil over a low heat. Pour the mixture over the fruit, stir and leave to cool.

4. Stir again, cover and chill in the refrigerator for at least 1 hour, stirring occasionally.

5. Divide the fruit salad equally between four bowls to serve.

GREEK-STYLE YOGURT WITH ORANGE ZEST & TOASTED SEEDS

SERVES: *2* | **PREP:** *5 mins* | **COOK:** *5 mins*

INGREDIENTS

2 tsp linseeds

2 tsp pumpkin seeds

2 tsp chia seeds

200 g/7 oz Greek-style natural yogurt

grated zest of 1 small orange

1 tsp orange juice

1. Heat a small frying pan over a medium heat.

2. Tip in the linseeds, pumpkin seeds and chia seeds. Toast, stirring constantly with a wooden spoon, until they start to turn brown and release a nutty aroma.

3. Tip the seeds onto a plate and leave to cool.

4. Spoon the yogurt into two glass pots or serving bowls, then scatter the seeds on top, followed by the orange zest.

5. Sprinkle over the orange juice and serve immediately.

QUINOA & CASHEW NUT PORRIDGE

INGREDIENTS

175 g/6 oz quinoa
25 g/1 oz cashew nuts, roughly
   chopped
1 litre/1¾ pints almond milk
1 vanilla pod, split and seeds
   removed
1 apple, grated
1 tsp ground cinnamon
1 tbsp maple syrup
2 tbsp chia seeds

TO SERVE

100 g/3½ oz raspberries
50 g/1¾ oz blueberries
2 tbsp pomegranate seeds

1. Place the quinoa in a pan with the cashew nuts, almond milk, vanilla seeds, apple, cinnamon and maple syrup.

2. Bring to the boil, then reduce the heat and simmer for 10–12 minutes. Stir the chia seeds into the pan and stir well.

3. Divide the porridge between four bowls and serve topped with the raspberries, blueberries and pomegranate seeds.

SUPERFOOD
BREAKFAST BARS

MAKES: *12 bars* | **PREP:** *10 mins, plus cooling* | **COOK:** *20–25 mins*

INGREDIENTS

20 g/¾ oz butter, for greasing

100 g/3½ oz coconut oil

100 g/3½ oz black treacle

20 g/¾ oz dark muscovado sugar

25 g/1 oz agave syrup

235 g/8½ oz rolled oats

50 g/1¾ oz pecan nuts, roughly
 chopped

50 g/1¾ oz cocoa nibs

50 g/1¾ oz blueberries

1. Preheat the oven to 180°C/350°F/Gas Mark 4. Grease an 18-cm/
7-inch square traybake tin.

2. Put the coconut oil, treacle, sugar and agave syrup into a large
saucepan and heat until melted. Stir until the sugar has dissolved,
then remove from the heat.

3. Stir in the remaining ingredients and mix them well together.

4. Pour into the prepared tin and level the top.

5. Bake in the preheated oven for 18–20 minutes, then leave to cool
in the tin for 5 minutes before cutting into squares.

6. Leave in the tin to cool completely.

7. Store in an airtight container for up to 5 days.

ORANGE & BANANA PANCAKES

INGREDIENTS

125 g/4½ oz teff flour
½ tsp ground cinnamon
1 tsp baking powder
1 egg
175 ml/6 fl oz milk
25 g/1 oz unsalted butter, melted
1 banana, peeled and diced
1 tbsp melted coconut oil

TO SERVE

2 oranges, peeled and segmented
1 tbsp sesame seeds, toasted
maple syrup (optional), for
*   drizzling*

1. Mix the flour, cinnamon and baking powder together in a large mixing bowl.

2. Whisk the egg and milk together in a separate bowl, then whisk into the flour mixture until smooth – the batter should be the consistency of thick double cream. Add a little more milk if needed.

3. Stir the melted butter and banana into the pancake batter.

4. Heat the coconut oil in a frying pan over a medium heat, then spoon in tablespoons of the batter. Cook for 3–4 minutes until the pancakes are golden underneath, then flip over and cook for a further 2–3 minutes.

5. Repeat with the remaining batter until you have 12 pancakes.

6. Serve the pancakes topped with the orange segments, a sprinkling of toasted sesame seeds and a drizzle of maple syrup, if using.

KALE GREEN
TROPIC JUICE

SERVES: *1* | **PREP:** *10–15 mins* | **COOK:** *No cooking*

INGREDIENTS

10 g/¼ oz kale

60 g/2¼ oz pineapple

15 g/½ oz spinach

½ tsp wheatgrass powder

3½ tbsp chilled water

1 pineapple segment, to garnish

1. Shred the kale and peel, core and roughly chop the pineapple. Add to a blender.

2. Add the spinach and wheatgrass powder to the blender. Pour over the chilled water and blend until smooth.

3. Pour into a glass and garnish with the pineapple segment. Serve immediately.

LINSEED & CHIA CHOCOLATE SMOOTHIE

SERVES: *2* | **PREP:** *5 mins* | **COOK:** *No cooking*

INGREDIENTS

300 ml/10 fl oz milk
1 banana
2 tsp milled linseeds
1 tsp milled chia seeds
3 tsp cacao powder
1 egg (optional)

1. Please note that infants, the elderly, pregnant women, convalescents and anyone suffering from an illness should avoid eating raw eggs.

2. Place the milk in a blender. Peel and chop the banana and add to the blender with the linseeds, chia seeds and cacao powder.

3. Add the egg, if using, and blend until smooth.

4. Pour the smoothie into two glasses and serve.

BERRY BOOSTER
JUICE

SERVES: *1* | **PREP:** *15 mins* | **COOK:** *No cooking*

INGREDIENTS

150 g/5½ oz strawberries
85 g/3 oz raspberries
85 g/3 oz blackberries
175 ml/6 fl oz chilled water

1. Cut a strawberry in half and reserve one half, along with a raspberry and a blackberry. Hull the remaining strawberries.

2. Put the strawberries, raspberries, blackberries and water in a blender and blend until smooth.

3. Pour the berry juice into a glass.

4. Thread the reserved fruit onto a wooden skewer to make a stirrer, then serve with the juice.

BANANA BREAKFAST SMOOTHIE

SERVES: *2* | **PREP:** *5 mins* | **COOK:** *No cooking*

INGREDIENTS

2 large ripe bananas

2 tbsp oat bran

2 tbsp honey

1 tbsp lemon juice

300 ml/10 fl oz soya milk

ground cinnamon, to serve
(optional)

1. Peel and chop the bananas. Put the bananas, bran, honey, lemon juice and soya milk into a blender and blend until smooth.

2. Pour the smoothie into two tall glasses.

3. Sprinkle with ground cinnamon, if using, and serve immediately.

LAYERED POWERBOWL SMOOTHIE

SERVES: *2* | **PREP:** *10–15 mins* | **COOK:** *No cooking*

INGREDIENTS

1 large mango, peeled and chopped
2 kiwi fruits, peeled and chopped
½ tsp chlorella powder
450 g/1 lb watermelon, peeled and
chopped (leave the seeds in for
additional vitamins)
1 tbsp ground almonds
1 tsp sesame seeds
2 tbsp granola
¼ tsp ground cinnamon

1. Place the mango in a small blender and process until smooth. Divide between two glass bowls. Rinse the blender.

2. Place the kiwi fruits and chlorella powder in the blender and process until smooth. Spoon the mixture over the layer of mango in the bowls. Rinse the blender.

3. Place the watermelon in the blender and process until smooth. Add the ground almonds and sesame seeds and process briefly to combine. Spoon over the kiwi mixture.

4. Sprinkle with the granola and ground cinnamon and serve.

CRUSHED EDAMAME &
AVOCADO TOASTS

SERVES: *4* | **PREP:** *10 mins* | **COOK:** *8–10 mins*

INGREDIENTS

*125 g/4½ oz frozen edamame
   beans, thawed*

3 tbsp sunflower seeds

8 slices sourdough bread

2 tbsp tahini paste

1 tbsp lime juice

*2 avocados, stoned, peeled and
   chopped*

½ small red onion, thinly sliced

salt and pepper (optional)

avocado oil, to serve

1. Place the edamame beans in a microwavable container and microwave for 4½ minutes. Leave to cool in the container for a few minutes before removing the beans.

2. Toast the sunflower seeds in a dry frying pan over a medium heat for 2–3 minutes.

3. Toast the bread on both sides.

4. Place the edamame beans in a bowl with the tahini, lime juice and avocado and roughly crush with a fork.

5. Spoon the edamame mixture onto the toasts, then sprinkle with the toasted seeds and slices of onion. Season to taste with salt and pepper, if using.

6. Drizzle with avocado oil to serve.

BAKED EGGS
WITH ASPARAGUS

SERVES: *2* | **PREP:** *10 mins* | **COOK:** *15 mins*

INGREDIENTS

1¼ tbsp extra virgin rapeseed oil

½ tsp paprika

1 garlic clove, crushed

¼ tsp sea salt

¼ tsp pepper

12 asparagus spears, woody ends
   removed

4 eggs

1 tomato, deseeded and diced

1 tbsp snipped fresh chives

1. Preheat the oven to 190°C/375°F/Gas Mark 5. In a small bowl, combine 1 tablespoon of the oil with all but a pinch of the paprika. Thoroughly stir in the garlic, salt and pepper.

2. Coat the asparagus spears thoroughly in the flavoured oil, then place in two shallow gratin dishes. Roast in the preheated oven for 7 minutes, or until nearly tender when pierced with a sharp knife.

3. Crack the eggs evenly over the asparagus and drizzle over any remaining seasoned oil. Return to the oven for 5 minutes, or until the whites are set and the yolks still runny.

4. Serve the eggs and asparagus with the diced tomatoes and chives sprinkled over the top. Drizzle with the remaining rapeseed oil and garnish with the remaining paprika.

WILD MUSHROOM OMELETTE

SERVES: *2* | **PREP:** *20 mins* | **COOK:** *15–20 mins*

INGREDIENTS

1 tsp extra virgin olive oil

1 small onion, cut into wedges

2–3 garlic cloves, crushed

85 g/3 oz mixed wild mushrooms, halved if large

85 g/3 oz closed-cup mushrooms, sliced

1 courgette, grated

2 eggs

2 egg whites

2 tbsp water

1 yellow pepper, deseeded and cut into strips

1 tbsp grated Parmesan-style vegetarian cheese (optional)

1 tbsp shredded fresh basil

salt and pepper (optional)

rocket, to garnish

wholemeal bread, to serve

1. Heat the oil in a large non-stick frying pan. Add the onion and garlic, cover and cook, stirring occasionally, for 3 minutes. Add the mushrooms and cook for a further 4–5 minutes, or until the mushrooms have softened slightly. Add the courgette.

2. Beat together the eggs, egg whites and water with salt and pepper to taste, if using.

3. Pour the egg mixture into the frying pan. Increase the heat slightly and cook, using a fork or spatula to draw the egg into the centre of the pan.

4. When the omelette is set on the base, sprinkle over the yellow pepper, the cheese, if using, and the basil. Cook for a further 3–4 minutes, or until set to your liking. Cut the omelette into wedges, garnish with rocket and serve with wholemeal bread.

PEA & KALE
FRITTATAS

MAKES: *12 frittatas* | **PREP:** *10 mins, plus cooling* | **COOK:** *25–30 mins*

INGREDIENTS

butter, for greasing
1 tbsp olive oil
4 spring onions, trimmed and
   chopped
100 g/3½ oz frozen peas, thawed
50 g/1¾ oz kale, shredded
6 eggs
100 ml/3½ fl oz milk
100 g/3½ oz vegetarian feta cheese,
   crumbled
salt and pepper (optional)

1. Preheat the oven to 180°C/350°F/Gas Mark 4. Grease a 12-hole muffin tin and set aside.

2. Heat the oil in a frying pan, add the spring onions and cook over a medium heat for 3–4 minutes until beginning to soften.

3. Add the peas and kale and cook for a further 2–3 minutes.

4. Beat the eggs and milk together in a bowl and season to taste with salt and pepper, if using.

5. Divide the pea and kale mixture between the holes in the prepared tin and pour some eggy milk over each one.

6. Sprinkle the cheese over the top of each frittata and bake in the preheated oven for 18–20 minutes until golden and set.

7. Leave the frittatas to cool in the tin for a few minutes, then remove them with a spatula. Serve warm or cold.

POACHED EGGS 'FLORENTINE' WITH SPINACH & CHEDDAR

SERVES: *4* | **PREP:** *15 mins* | **COOK:** *13–15 mins*

INGREDIENTS

1 tbsp olive oil
200 g/7 oz young spinach leaves
4 thick slices ciabatta bread
25 g/1 oz butter
4 large eggs
100 g/3½ oz vegetarian Cheddar
  cheese, grated
salt and pepper (optional)
freshly grated nutmeg, to serve

1. Preheat the grill to high. Heat the oil in a wok or large saucepan, add the spinach and stir-fry for 2–3 minutes until the leaves are wilted. Drain in a colander, season to taste with salt and pepper, if using, and keep warm.

2. Toast the bread on both sides until golden. Spread one side of each slice with butter and place buttered side up on a baking sheet.

3. Add a little salt, if using, to a small saucepan of water and bring to the boil. Crack the eggs into the water and poach for about 3 minutes until the whites are set but the yolks still runny. Remove from the pan with a draining spoon.

4. Arrange the spinach on the toast and top each slice with a poached egg. Sprinkle with the grated cheese. Cook under the preheated grill for 1–2 minutes until the cheese has melted. Sprinkle with nutmeg and serve immediately.

EGGS WITH FRIED TOMATO, ONION & PEPPERS

SERVES: *4* | **PREP:** *10 mins* | **COOK:** *30 mins*

INGREDIENTS

4 large ripe tomatoes

1½ tbsp rapeseed oil

1 large onion, finely chopped

½ tsp coriander seeds, crushed

½ tsp caraway seeds, crushed

2 red peppers, deseeded and diced

¼ tsp dried chilli flakes

1 large garlic clove, thinly sliced

4 eggs

sea salt and pepper (optional)

chopped fresh flat-leaf parsley, to garnish

1. Put the tomatoes into a shallow bowl and cover with boiling water. Leave to stand for 30 seconds, then drain.

2. Slip off the tomato skins and discard. Chop the flesh, reserving the seeds and juice.

3. Heat the oil in a large, non-stick frying pan over a medium heat. Add the onion, coriander seeds and caraway seeds. Fry, stirring occasionally, for about 10 minutes until the onion is soft and golden.

4. Stir in the red peppers and chilli flakes and fry for about 5 minutes until soft.

5. Add the garlic and tomatoes with their seeds and juices and season to taste with salt and pepper, if using. Simmer, uncovered, over a low heat for 10 minutes.

6. Crack the eggs over the surface. Cover and cook for a further 3–4 minutes, or until the eggs are set. Season to taste with salt and pepper, if using, sprinkle with parsley and serve immediately.

ASPARAGUS &
PEA FRITTATA

SERVES: *4* | **PREP:** *15 mins* | **COOK:** *20-25 mins*

INGREDIENTS

8 asparagus spears

350 g/12 oz peas, shelled

8 eggs

½ tsp sea salt

1 tbsp olive oil

large knob of butter

8 spring onions, trimmed and finely
   sliced

pepper (optional)

1. Snap the woody ends from the asparagus and discard. Chop
the stems into 1-cm/½-inch pieces and chop the tips into 2.5-cm/
1-inch pieces.

2. Put the asparagus and peas into a steamer basket set over a
saucepan of boiling water. Steam for 3 minutes. Remove from the
heat and set aside.

3. Beat the eggs well. Add the salt and some pepper, if using.

4. Heat the oil and butter in a 24-cm/9½-inch non-stick frying pan
over a medium heat. Add the spring onions and fry for 2 minutes.
Stir in the peas and asparagus. Pour in the eggs, stirring to distribute
the vegetables evenly.

5. Cover the pan and cook over a medium–low heat for 10–12
minutes, or until the eggs are almost set. Place under a hot grill and
cook for a further 3–5 minutes, or until the top is set. Turn out onto a
plate and cut into wedges. Serve hot or warm.

MUSHROOMS & SIZZLED SAGE ON SOURDOUGH TOAST

SERVES: *4* | **PREP:** *15 mins* | **COOK:** *10 mins*

INGREDIENTS

5 tbsp olive oil

*2 tbsp roughly chopped fresh sage,
plus 16–20 whole small leaves*

*400 g/14 oz even-sized chestnut
mushrooms, halved*

lemon juice

1 large garlic clove, thinly sliced

*2 tbsp chopped fresh flat-leaf
parsley*

¼ tsp pepper

pinch of sea salt flakes

4 slices sourdough bread

*Parmesan-style vegetarian cheese
shavings, to garnish*

1. Heat the oil in a large frying pan over a medium–high heat. Add the chopped sage and sizzle for a few seconds. Add the mushrooms and fry for 3–4 minutes until they begin to release their juices.

2. Add a squeeze of lemon juice, then add the garlic, parsley, pepper and salt. Cook for a further 5 minutes.

3. Meanwhile, toast the bread on both sides. Place on warmed plates and pile the mushrooms on top. Sizzle the whole sage leaves in the oil remaining in the pan over a high heat for a few seconds, until crisp. Scatter over the mushrooms. Sprinkle over some cheese shavings and serve immediately.

CHAPTER TWO

SOUPS & SALADS

LENTIL &
CHICKPEA SOUP

SERVES: *4* | **PREP:** *10 mins* | **COOK:** *30 mins*

INGREDIENTS

150 g/5½ oz brown rice
2 tsp cumin seeds
¼ tsp chilli flakes
1½ tbsp melted coconut oil, for
    frying
1 red onion, chopped
140 g/5 oz red split lentils
900 ml/1½ pints vegetable stock
400 g/14 oz canned chopped
    tomatoes
200 g/7 oz canned chickpeas,
    drained and rinsed
4 spring onions, trimmed and sliced
200 g/7 oz canned Puy lentils,
    drained and rinsed
salt and pepper (optional)
Greek-style natural yogurt and
    fresh coriander leaves, to serve

1. Cook the rice according to the packet instructions.

2. Meanwhile, fry the cumin seeds and chilli flakes in a dry saucepan over a medium heat for 1 minute, then add 1 tablespoon of the coconut oil.

3. Add the onion to the pan and cook for 3–4 minutes. Stir in the red split lentils, stock, tomatoes and half the chickpeas and bring to the boil. Simmer for 15 minutes, until the lentils are soft.

4. Meanwhile, heat the remaining oil in a separate saucepan and sauté the spring onions over a medium heat for 3–4 minutes, then stir in the Puy lentils. Cook for 1–2 minutes to heat through.

5. Using a hand-held blender, blend the soup in the pan until smooth. Season to taste with salt and pepper, if using.

6. Pour the soup into four warmed bowls and add a spoonful each of rice, the remaining chickpeas, the spring onions and Puy lentils to each one. Serve topped with a dollop of yogurt and a sprinkling of coriander leaves.

BROAD BEAN
& MINT SOUP

SERVES: 4 | **PREP:** 20 mins | **COOK:** 15 mins

INGREDIENTS

1 kg/2 lb 4 oz broad beans, shelled
   (300 g/10½ oz shelled weight)
2 tbsp olive oil
1 onion, finely chopped
400 ml/14 fl oz hot vegetable stock
2 garlic cloves, finely chopped
grated zest and juice of ½ unwaxed
   lemon
25 g/1 oz fresh mint leaves
pinch of sea salt
pinch of pepper
4 tbsp Greek-style natural yogurt

1. Put the beans in a heatproof bowl and pour over just enough boiling water to cover. Drain well and immediately plunge them into a bowl of cold water. Peel off and discard the outer skins and set the beans aside.

2. Meanwhile, heat the oil in a large saucepan over a low heat. Add the onion, cover and cook for 10 minutes, stirring occasionally, until translucent. Add the beans, reserving a small handful, stir briefly, then pour in 300 ml/10 fl oz of the stock. Bring to the boil, then simmer for 2 minutes, or until the beans are tender.

3. Stir in the garlic, lemon zest and half the mint. Whizz in a food processor or with a hand-held blender until smooth. Check the consistency – if you prefer a thinner soup, mix in a little or all of the reserved stock. Stir in the lemon juice, salt and pepper.

4. Pour the soup into four shallow bowls. Swirl a tablespoon of yogurt into each bowl, then scatter with the reserved beans, tear over the remaining mint leaves and serve.

TOMATO
SOUP

SERVES: *4* | **PREP:** *15 mins* | **COOK:** *35 mins*

INGREDIENTS

25 g/1 oz butter

2 tbsp olive oil

1 large onion, finely chopped

2 garlic cloves, finely chopped

1 celery stick, finely chopped

500 g/1 lb 2 oz plum tomatoes,
*   peeled, cored and chopped*

2 tbsp tomato purée

100 ml/3½ fl oz water

brown sugar, to taste

1 tbsp chopped fresh basil, plus
*   extra to garnish*

300 ml/10 fl oz vegetable stock

salt and pepper (optional)

1. Melt the butter with the oil in a saucepan. Add the onion, garlic and celery and cook over a low heat, stirring occasionally, for 5 minutes until soft. Stir in the tomatoes, tomato purée and water. Increase the heat to medium and bring to the boil, then reduce the heat and simmer, stirring occasionally, for 10 minutes.

2. Increase the heat to medium, then stir in sugar to taste, the basil and stock. Season to taste with salt and pepper, if using. Bring to the boil, then reduce the heat and simmer for a further 10 minutes.

3. Taste and adjust the seasoning with salt and pepper, if using. Ladle into warmed bowls, garnish with basil and serve immediately.

CREAM OF
MUSHROOM SOUP

SERVES: *4* | **PREP:** *15 mins, plus cooling* | **COOK:** *1 hour 40 mins–1 hour 50 mins*

INGREDIENTS

115 g/4 oz unsalted butter

900 g/2 lb white button mushrooms,
thickly sliced

1 onion, roughly chopped

1 tbsp flour

1 litre/1¾ pints vegetable stock

225 ml/8 fl oz water

6 fresh thyme sprigs, plus extra
leaves to garnish

3 garlic cloves

225 ml/8 fl oz double cream

salt and pepper (optional)

1. Melt the butter in a large saucepan over a medium heat. Add the mushrooms and a pinch of salt. Cook, stirring occasionally, for 20–30 minutes, or until the mushrooms are golden brown. Reserve some mushrooms to garnish the soup.

2. Add the onion and cook over a medium–low heat for about 5 minutes. Add the flour and cook, stirring, for 1 minute. Whisk in the stock and water. Add the thyme and garlic and bring to a simmer. Reduce the heat to low, cover and simmer gently for 1 hour.

3. Remove the soup from the heat, uncover and leave to cool for 15 minutes. Transfer to a food processor or blender, in batches if necessary, and process until smooth.

4. Return the soup to the rinsed-out pan and gently reheat; do not boil. Add the cream, taste and adjust the seasoning with a little salt and pepper, if using. Serve hot, topped with the reserved mushrooms and some thyme leaves.

ROAST MEDITERRANEAN VEGETABLE SOUP

SERVES: *6* | **PREP:** *15 mins* | **COOK:** *2 hours 5 mins, plus cooling*

INGREDIENTS

2 aubergines

4 tomatoes

2 red peppers

2 onions, unpeeled

2 garlic cloves, unpeeled

4 tbsp olive oil, plus extra for
    drizzling

1 fresh oregano sprig

1.5 litres/2½ pints vegetable stock

salt and pepper (optional)

4 tsp chopped fresh basil, to garnish

1. Preheat the oven to 180°C/350°F/Gas Mark 4. Prick the aubergines several times with a fork and put in a roasting tin. Add the tomatoes, peppers and unpeeled onions and garlic. Sprinkle with 2 tablespoons of the oil. Roast in the preheated oven for 30 minutes, then remove the tomatoes. Roast the aubergines, peppers, onions and garlic for a further 30 minutes, until very soft and the pepper skins have blackened.

2. Put the cooked roasted vegetables in a bowl, cover with a damp tea towel and leave for 3–4 hours or overnight, until cold. When cold, cut the aubergines in half, scoop out the flesh and put in the bowl. Remove the skin from the tomatoes, cut in half and discard the seeds and add the flesh to the bowl. Hold the peppers over the bowl to collect the juices and peel off the skin. Remove the stem, core and seeds and add the flesh to the bowl. Peel the onions, cut into quarters and add to the bowl. Squeeze the garlic cloves out of their skin into the bowl.

3. Heat the remaining oil in a large saucepan. Add the vegetables and their juices, the leaves from the oregano sprig, and salt and pepper, if using, then cook gently, stirring frequently, for 30 minutes. Add the stock and bring to the boil, then simmer for 30 minutes.

4. Remove the saucepan from the heat and leave to cool slightly. Transfer to a food processor or blender, in batches if necessary, and process until smooth. Return the soup to the rinsed-out pan and reheat gently; do not boil. Ladle into warmed bowls, drizzle with a little oil, garnish with basil and serve immediately.

YELLOW TOMATO GAZPACHO

SERVES: *4–6* | **PREP:** *30–35 mins, plus chilling* | **COOK:** *No cooking*

INGREDIENTS

900 g/2 lb large yellow tomatoes, halved

½ cucumber, peeled, deseeded and diced

1 yellow pepper, deseeded and diced

100 g/3½ oz red cherry tomatoes, deseeded and chopped

3 large spring onions, finely chopped

1–2 green chillies, deseeded and finely chopped

2 tbsp wine vinegar

3 tbsp extra virgin olive oil, plus extra for drizzling

4 garlic cloves

½ tsp sea salt flakes, plus extra to taste

¼ tsp pepper, plus extra to taste

¼ tsp sugar

small handful basil leaves, shredded, to garnish

ready-made garlic croûtons, to serve

1. Scoop out the seeds and juice from the yellow tomatoes. Pass the seeds and juice through a sieve set over a bowl. Chop the flesh and add to the bowl. Set aside 4 tablespoons each of the cucumber and yellow pepper. Set aside all of the chopped cherry tomatoes.

2. Add the remaining cucumber and yellow pepper to the yellow tomatoes. Add the onions, chilli, vinegar and oil. Tip into a food processor and process, frequently scraping down the side of the bowl, for 2 minutes until very smooth. Pour back into the bowl.

3. Put the garlic into a mortar with the salt and crush with a pestle. Stir into the tomato mixture with the pepper and sugar. Chill for several hours until really cold.

4. Check the seasoning, adding more salt and pepper to taste. Ladle into chilled bowls. Top with the reserved yellow pepper, the cucumber and the cherry tomatoes. Add a slick of oil and a few shredded basil leaves and serve with garlic croûtons.

PEA & HERB SOUP
WITH BASIL OIL

SERVES: *4* | **PREP:** *20 mins, plus cooling* | **COOK:** *25 mins*

INGREDIENTS

25 g/1 oz butter

6 spring onions, chopped

1 celery stick, finely chopped

375 g/13 oz frozen peas or fresh shelled peas

750 ml/1¼ pints vegetable stock

2 tbsp chopped fresh dill

1 tbsp snipped fresh chives

35 g/1¼ oz rocket leaves

2 tbsp crème fraîche

salt and pepper (optional)

bread sticks, to serve

BASIL OIL

25 g/1 oz fresh basil sprigs

200 ml/7 fl oz olive oil

1. Melt the butter in a saucepan over a medium heat. Add the spring onions and celery, cover and cook for 5 minutes until soft. Add the peas and stock, bring to the boil and simmer for 10 minutes. Remove from the heat. Cover and leave to cool for 20 minutes.

2. To make the basil oil, remove the stems from the basil and discard. Place the leaves in a food processor with half the oil and blend to a purée. Add the remaining oil and blend again. Transfer to a small bowl and set aside.

3. Add the dill, chives and rocket to the soup. Blend with a hand-held blender until smooth. Stir in the crème fraîche. If serving warm, heat through gently without boiling, then season to taste.

4. Ladle into four warmed bowls and drizzle with the basil oil. Serve immediately, with bread sticks on the side. If serving chilled, leave to cool completely, then chill in the refrigerator for at least 1 hour. Taste and adjust the seasoning with salt and pepper, if using, then serve.

LEEK & SPINACH
SOUP

SERVES: *4* | **PREP:** *20 mins* | **COOK:** *45 mins*

INGREDIENTS

25 g/1 oz butter

2 leeks, trimmed, halved
lengthways and thinly sliced

225 g/8 oz potatoes, cut into bite-
sized chunks

300 g/10½ oz spinach, stalks
discarded, leaves sliced

300 ml/10 fl oz hot vegetable stock

1 tsp lemon juice

pinch of freshly grated nutmeg

sea salt and pepper (optional)

soured cream, to serve

1. Melt the butter in a large saucepan over a medium–low heat. Add the leeks and potatoes, cover and cook for 10 minutes, or until beginning to soften.

2. Stir in two thirds of the spinach. Cover and cook for 2–3 minutes until starting to wilt. Season with salt and pepper, if using, and stir in half the stock. Bring to the boil, then simmer for 20 minutes, partially covered.

3. Transfer half the soup to a food processor and process until smooth. Return to the pan.

4. Purée the remaining uncooked spinach and the remaining stock. Add to the soup in the pan. Stir in the lemon juice and nutmeg and gently reheat.

5. Ladle into warmed bowls, swirl in a spoonful of soured cream and serve immediately.

BROCCOLI & STILTON SOUP

SERVES: *4–6* | **PREP:** *20 mins, plus cooling* | **COOK:** *40–45 mins*

INGREDIENTS

40 g/1½ oz butter

2 onions, chopped

1 large potato, chopped

750 g/1 lb 10 oz broccoli florets

1.5 litres/2½ pints vegetable stock

150 g/5½ oz vegetarian Stilton
cheese, diced

pinch of ground mace

salt and pepper (optional)

ready-made croûtons, to garnish

1. Melt the butter in a large saucepan. Add the onions and potato and stir well. Cover and cook over a low heat for 7 minutes. Add the broccoli and stir, then re-cover and cook for a further 5 minutes.

2. Increase the heat to medium, pour in the stock and bring to the boil. Reduce the heat, season to taste with salt and pepper, if using, and re-cover. Simmer for 15–20 minutes until all the vegetables are tender.

3. Remove the pan from the heat and strain the contents into a bowl, reserving the vegetables, then leave to cool slightly. Put the vegetables into a food processor, add 1 ladleful of the stock and process to a smooth purée. With the motor running, gradually add the remaining stock.

4. Return the soup to the rinsed-out pan and reheat gently, but do not allow to boil. Remove from the heat and stir in the cheese until melted and thoroughly combined. Stir in the mace and taste and adjust the seasoning with a little salt and pepper, if using. Ladle into warmed serving bowls, sprinkle with the croûtons and serve.

SWEET POTATO
& APPLE SOUP

SERVES: 6 | **PREP:** 20 mins, plus cooling | **COOK:** 50 mins

INGREDIENTS

1 tbsp butter
3 leeks, thinly sliced
1 large carrot, thinly sliced
600 g/1 lb 5 oz sweet potatoes,
*   peeled and diced*
2 large Bramley apples, peeled,
*   cored and diced*
1.2 litres/2 pints water
pinch of freshly grated nutmeg
225 ml/8 fl oz apple juice
225 ml/8 fl oz single cream
salt and pepper (optional)
snipped fresh chives or chopped
*   fresh coriander, to garnish*

1. Melt the butter in a large saucepan over a medium–low heat.

2. Add the leeks, cover and cook for 6–8 minutes, or until soft, stirring frequently.

3. Add the carrot, sweet potatoes, apples and water. Add the nutmeg and season to taste with salt and pepper, if using. Bring to the boil, reduce the heat and simmer, covered, for about 20 minutes, stirring occasionally, until the vegetables are very tender. Leave to cool slightly in the pan, then purée with a hand-held blender.

4. Stir in the apple juice, place over a low heat and simmer for about 10 minutes until heated through.

5. Stir in the cream and simmer for a further 5 minutes, stirring frequently, until heated through. Taste and adjust the seasoning with a little salt and pepper, if using.

6. Ladle the soup into six warmed bowls, garnish with chives and serve immediately.

LEEK & POTATO SOUP

SERVES: *6* | **PREP:** *15 mins* | **COOK:** *30 mins*

INGREDIENTS

55 g/2 oz butter

1 onion, chopped

3 leeks, sliced

225 g/8 oz potatoes, cut into
*   2-cm/¾-inch cubes*

900 ml/1½ pints vegetable stock

salt and pepper (optional)

snipped fresh chives, to garnish

single cream and crusty bread,
*   to serve*

1. Melt the butter in a large saucepan over a medium heat, add the onion, leeks and potatoes and sauté gently for 2–3 minutes until soft but not brown. Pour in the stock, bring to the boil, then reduce the heat and simmer, covered, for 15 minutes.

2. Process using a hand-held blender, until smooth.

3. Heat the soup gently over a low heat, then season to taste with a little salt and pepper, if using. Ladle into warmed bowls, add a swirl of cream, garnish with snipped chives and serve immediately with some crusty bread.

SEAWEED POWER BOWL

SERVES: *4* | **PREP:** *20 mins* | **COOK:** *No cooking*

INGREDIENTS

20 g/¾ oz dried kelp

½ cucumber

2 oranges

1 red chilli, deseeded and finely diced

2 carrots, grated

1 large mango, peeled, stoned and chopped

3 heads of pak choi, chopped

15 g/½ oz fresh coriander leaves

2 tbsp salted peanuts, chopped

DRESSING

3 tbsp olive oil

grated zest and juice of 1 lime

1 tsp clear honey

1 tsp miso paste

1. Place the kelp in a bowl of water and leave to stand for 10 minutes to rehydrate.

2. Meanwhile, to make the dressing, whisk together the oil, lime zest and juice, honey and miso paste.

3. Halve the cucumber lengthways and, using a teaspoon, scoop out and discard the seeds. Slice the cucumber.

4. Peel the oranges and cut them into segments.

5. Roughly chop the drained kelp and place in a large bowl with the cucumber, orange segments, chilli, carrots, mango, pak choi and half the coriander.

6. Pour in the dressing and toss well. Divide between four bowls and sprinkle with chopped peanuts and the remaining coriander.

RAW BEETROOT
& PECAN SALAD

SERVES: *4* | **PREP:** *15–20 mins* | **COOK:** *No cooking*

INGREDIENTS

175 g/6 oz fresh beetroot, coarsely
grated
8 radishes, thinly sliced
2 spring onions, finely chopped
25 g/1 oz pecan nuts, roughly
chopped
red chicory leaves or Little Gem
lettuce leaves

DRESSING

2 tbsp extra virgin olive oil
1 tbsp balsamic vinegar
2 tsp creamed horseradish sauce
salt and pepper (optional)

1. Combine the beetroot, radishes, spring onions and pecan nuts in a bowl and toss well to mix evenly.

2. Place all the dressing ingredients in a small bowl and lightly whisk with a fork. Season to taste with salt and pepper, if using, and pour over the vegetables in the bowl, tossing to coat evenly.

3. Arrange the chicory leaves on a serving platter and spoon the salad over them.

4. Serve the salad cold on its own or as an accompaniment.

BORLOTTI BEAN, TOMATO & ONION SALAD WITH EGGS

SERVES: *4* | **PREP:** *25 mins, plus soaking* | **COOK:** *1 hour 45 mins–2 hours 15 mins*

INGREDIENTS

*250 g/9 oz dried borlotti beans,
   soaked in cold water for 5 hours,
   or overnight*
2 large garlic cloves, crushed
juice of 2 lemons
6 tbsp extra virgin olive oil
1 tsp salt
1 small onion, finely diced
*2 tomatoes, deseeded and finely
   diced*
*about 40 g/1½ oz fresh flat-leaf
   parsley, thick stems removed,
   leaves chopped*
1 tsp cumin seeds, crushed
pepper (optional)
warmed pittas, to serve

TO GARNISH

4 hard-boiled eggs, quartered
4 lemon wedges
sumac or crushed red pepper flakes

1. Drain the beans, rinse well and put into a large saucepan. Cover with water and bring to the boil. Boil for 10 minutes, then reduce the heat and simmer for 1½–2 hours, or until very tender. Top up with boiling water if necessary.

2. Drain the beans and tip into a shallow serving dish. Lightly crush some of them with the back of a wooden spoon.

3. Add the garlic, lemon juice, oil and salt while the beans are still warm. Mix gently, then add the onion, tomatoes and parsley. Add the cumin seeds and some pepper, if using, and gently toss.

4. Arrange the egg quarters and lemon wedges on top. Sprinkle with a pinch of sumac. Serve with fingers of pitta.

BLACK RICE & POMEGRANATE BOWL

INGREDIENTS

1 small butternut squash, peeled,
deseeded and diced

1 red onion, sliced

1 tbsp olive oil

125 g/4½ oz black rice

70 g/2½ oz kale, shredded

2 tbsp pine nuts

400 g/14 oz canned butter beans,
drained and rinsed

vegetarian cottage cheese and
pomegranate seeds, to serve

DRESSING

4 tbsp tahini paste

juice of 1 lemon

1 garlic clove, crushed

2 tbsp extra virgin olive oil

1. Preheat the oven to 200°C/400°F/Gas Mark 6.

2. Place the butternut squash and onion in a roasting tin and drizzle with the olive oil. Roast in the preheated oven for 15 minutes.

3. Cook the rice according to the packet instructions.

4. Meanwhile, add the kale and pine nuts to the squash and roast for a further 10 minutes. Remove from the oven, add the butter beans and toss.

5. To make the dressing, whisk the tahini, lemon juice, garlic and extra virgin olive oil together in a small bowl. Set aside.

6. Drain the rice and divide between four warmed bowls. Spoon over the roasted vegetables and nuts, a dollop of cottage cheese and a sprinkling of pomegranate seeds.

7. Drizzle the dressing into each bowl to serve.

CARROT, COCONUT
& MANGO SALAD

SERVES: *2–3* | **PREP:** *25 mins, plus standing* | **COOK:** *No cooking*

INGREDIENTS

350 g/12 oz young carrots, scrubbed

1 ripe mango, about 375 g/13 oz,
*   peeled and cut into small cubes*

55 g/2 oz fresh coconut flesh, very
*   thinly sliced*

3 tbsp chopped fresh coriander

3 tbsp toasted skinned hazelnuts,
*   roughly chopped*

½ tsp muscovado sugar

½ tsp sea salt flakes

finely grated rind of 1 lime

lime segments, to garnish

DRESSING

1 tsp muscovado sugar

¼ tsp sea salt

juice of 1 lime

¼–½ small green chilli, deseeded
*   and very finely chopped*

3 tbsp hazelnut oil or light olive oil

pepper (optional)

1. Cut the carrots into 5-cm/2-inch lengths. Using a swivel peeler, shave into wide ribbons, discarding the woody core. Put into a shallow dish and add the mango and coconut.

2. To make the dressing, dissolve the sugar and salt in the lime juice. Stir in the chilli and add pepper to taste, if using. Add the oil and whisk until smooth.

3. Pour the dressing over the carrot mixture, tossing well. Leave to stand at room temperature for 20 minutes until the flavours develop.

4. Add the coriander and toss again. Mix the hazelnuts with the sugar, salt and lime rind.

5. Arrange the mixture on individual serving plates and sprinkle with the nut mixture. Garnish with lime segments and serve immediately.

BROCCOLI
SALAD

SERVES: *4* | **PREP:** *20 mins* | **COOK:** *10–15 mins*

INGREDIENTS

200 g/7 oz purple sprouting broccoli

250 g/9 oz red cabbage, shredded

115 g/4 oz cooked beetroot in
   natural juices (drained weight),
   drained and cut into matchsticks

2 tbsp dried cranberries

3 tbsp balsamic vinegar

CROÛTONS

2 tbsp olive oil

85 g/3 oz rustic wholegrain bread,
   torn into small pieces

1 tbsp sunflower seeds

1 tbsp linseeds

1. Put the broccoli in the top of a steamer, cover and set over a saucepan of simmering water. Steam for 3–5 minutes, or until tender. Cool under cold running water, cut the stems in half, then cut the lower stems in half again lengthways and transfer them to a salad bowl.

2. Add the red cabbage, beetroot and dried cranberries to the bowl.

3. To make the croûtons, heat the oil in a frying pan over a medium heat, add the bread and fry for 3–4 minutes, stirring, until just beginning to brown. Add the sunflower seeds and linseeds and cook for a further 2–3 minutes until lightly toasted.

4. Drizzle the vinegar over the salad and gently toss together. Sprinkle with the croûtons and seeds and serve immediately.

RADICCHIO &
RED PEPPER SALAD

SERVES: *4* | **PREP:** *15 mins* | **COOK:** *No cooking*

INGREDIENTS

2 red peppers

1 head of radicchio, separated into
*   leaves*

4 whole cooked beetroot, cut into
*   matchsticks*

12 radishes, sliced

4 spring onions, finely chopped

4 tbsp ready-made vegetarian
*   salad dressing*

crusty bread, to serve

1. Core and deseed the red peppers and cut into rounds.

2. Arrange the radicchio leaves in a salad bowl. Add the peppers, beetroots, radishes and spring onions.

3. Drizzle with the dressing, toss well and serve with crusty bread.

RAINBOW
SALAD

SERVES: *4* | **PREP:** *20 mins* | **COOK:** *6–8 mins*

INGREDIENTS

200 g/7 oz vegetarian halloumi
  cheese
40 g/1½ oz rocket
1 mango, peeled, stoned and
  chopped
12 cherry tomatoes, halved
1 yellow pepper, deseeded and
  sliced
35 g/1¼ oz mangetout, shredded
4 spring onions, thinly sliced
50 g/1¾ oz blueberries
35 g/1¼ oz sunflower seeds, toasted
35 g/1¼ oz pumpkin seeds, toasted
25 g/1 oz alfalfa sprouts

DRESSING

3 tbsp olive oil
juice of 1 lemon
1 tsp clear honey
1 tsp mustard

1. To make the dressing, whisk together the oil, lemon juice, honey and mustard.

2. Slice the cheese, add to a dry frying pan and cook for 3–4 minutes on each side until golden.

3. Divide the rocket between four bowls, then top with the mango, tomatoes, yellow pepper, mangetout, spring onions and blueberries.

4. Top each serving with slices of cheese and sprinkle with the sunflower seeds, pumpkin seeds and alfalfa sprouts.

5. Drizzle over the dressing and serve immediately.

WATERCRESS, COURGETTE & MINT SALAD

SERVES: *4* | **PREP:** *15 mins, plus cooling* | **COOK:** *12 mins*

INGREDIENTS

2 courgettes, cut into batons

100 g/3½ oz French beans, cut into thirds

1 green pepper, deseeded and cut into strips

2 celery sticks, sliced

1 bunch watercress

salt (optional)

DRESSING

200 ml/7 fl oz natural yogurt

1 garlic clove, crushed

2 tbsp chopped fresh mint

pepper (optional)

1. Add a little salt, if using, to a saucepan of water and bring to the boil. Add the courgette batons and beans, bring back to the boil and cook for 7–8 minutes.

2. Drain, rinse under cold running water and drain again. Set aside and leave to cool completely.

3. Mix the courgettes and beans with the green pepper strips, celery and watercress in a large serving bowl.

4. To make the dressing, combine the yogurt, garlic and mint in a small bowl. Season to taste with pepper, if using, toss with the salad and serve immediately.

CHUNKY AVOCADO
& SWEETCORN SALAD

SERVES: *4* | **PREP:** *20 mins* | **COOK:** *5 mins*

INGREDIENTS

200 g/7 oz frozen sweetcorn
1 large avocado, halved, stoned,
peeled and cut into cubes
175 g/6 oz cherry tomatoes, cut into
quarters
½ red onion, finely chopped
1 small green pepper, halved,
deseeded and cut into small
chunks
40 g/1½ oz kale, shredded
25 g/1 oz fresh coriander, roughly
chopped

DRESSING

finely grated rind and juice of
1 lime
2 tbsp olive oil
salt and pepper (optional)

1. Bring a saucepan of water to the boil. Add the sweetcorn, bring back to the boil, then simmer for 3 minutes. Drain into a colander, rinse with cold water, drain again, then transfer to a salad bowl.

2. To make the dressing, put the lime rind and juice and oil in a jam jar, season to taste with salt and pepper, if using, screw on the lid and shake well.

3. Add the avocado, tomatoes, onion, green pepper, kale and coriander to the sweetcorn, drizzle over the dressing and toss together. Spoon into four bowls and serve immediately.

CHAPTER THREE

LUNCH

FLATBREAD PIZZA WITH GARLIC COURGETTE RIBBONS

SERVES: *2* | **PREP:** *20 mins* | **COOK:** *10 mins*

INGREDIENTS

50 g/1¾ oz crème fraîche

150 g/5½ oz courgettes, shredded into ribbons using a vegetable peeler

55 g/2 oz cherry tomatoes, quartered

50 g/1¾ oz vegetarian ricotta cheese

1 garlic clove, crushed

2 tbsp olive oil

PIZZA BASES

100 g/3½ oz wholemeal plain flour, plus extra for dusting

50 g/1¾ oz quinoa flour

¾ tsp bicarbonate of soda

1 tbsp olive oil

2 tbsp lukewarm water

sea salt (optional)

1. Preheat the oven to 200°C/400°F/Gas Mark 6. To make the pizza bases, put the wholemeal flour, quinoa flour and bicarbonate of soda in a mixing bowl, add a little salt, if using, and stir to combine. Add the oil, then gradually mix in enough of the water to make a soft but not sticky dough.

2. Turn out the dough onto a work surface lightly dusted with wholemeal flour. Knead for 2 minutes, or until the dough is smooth and slightly elastic.

3. Put two large baking sheets in the preheated oven to heat.

4. Divide the dough into two pieces. Roll out each piece to a round about 5 mm/¼ inch thick. Remove the baking sheets from the oven and, working quickly, lay the dough on top. Spread the crème fraîche over the dough, then sprinkle with the courgettes and tomatoes. Blob small dollops of the ricotta cheese on top.

5. Bake the pizzas for 7–10 minutes, or until the crust is crispy and slightly puffed up, and the ricotta is tinged golden.

6. Mix the garlic and oil together in a jug and drizzle over the pizzas just before serving.

NEW POTATO, ROSEMARY
& ROCKET PIZZA

SERVES: *4* | **PREP:** *15 mins* | **COOK:** *25 mins*

INGREDIENTS

280 g/10 oz small waxy new
*   potatoes, unpeeled*
2 tbsp olive oil, plus extra for
*   greasing*
2 garlic cloves, thinly sliced
1½ tbsp chopped fresh rosemary
*   leaves*
1 ready-made 30-cm/12-inch pizza
*   base*
85 g/3 oz vegetarian smoked cheese,
*   coarsely grated*
115 g/4 oz vegetarian Gruyère
*   cheese, coarsely grated*
8 Kalamata olives, stoned and
*   halved*
handful of rocket
sea salt and pepper (optional)

1. Preheat the oven to 240°C/475°F/Gas Mark 9. Add a little salt, if using, to a saucepan of water and bring to the boil. Add the potatoes, bring back to the boil and blanch for 3 minutes. Drain the potatoes, then thinly slice.

2. Heat the oil in a large frying pan over a medium–high heat. Add the potatoes and fry for 3–4 minutes until lightly browned. Add the garlic, 1 tablespoon of the rosemary, and salt and pepper to taste, if using. Fry for a further 1 minute.

3. Place the pizza base on a baking sheet and sprinkle with two thirds of the smoked cheese and two thirds of the Gruyère cheese. Arrange the potatoes on top. Add the remaining cheese, the olives and the remaining rosemary.

4. Bake in the preheated oven for 10 minutes until lightly browned. Scatter over the rocket and serve immediately.

BRUSCHETTA WITH BROAD BEANS, MINT & GOAT'S CHEESE

SERVES: *6* | **PREP:** *25 mins* | **COOK:** *10 mins*

INGREDIENTS

600 g/1 lb 5 oz shelled small broad
   beans (about 2.5 kg/5 lb 8 oz
   unshelled weight)
3 tbsp extra virgin olive oil, plus
   extra for drizzling
1 tbsp lemon juice
1 tbsp chopped fresh mint leaves
6 slices ciabatta
1 large garlic clove, halved
6 tbsp soft fresh vegetarian goat's
   cheese
sea salt flakes and pepper
   (optional)

1. Add a little salt to a large saucepan of water and bring to the boil. Add the beans, bring back to the boil and cook for 3 minutes until just tender. Rinse under cold running water and drain.

2. Slip off the bean skins and discard.

3. Toss the beans with the oil, lemon juice and most of the mint. Season with a little salt and pepper, if using.

4. Tip the bean mixture into a food processor. Process briefly to a chunky purée.

5. Toast the bread on both sides. While the bread is still warm, rub one side of each slice with the cut garlic clove. Drizzle with oil.

6. Cut each bread slice in half. Spread with the bean mixture, top with a little goat's cheese and the remaining mint.

LEEK & GOAT'S CHEESE TARTLETS

SERVES: *6* | **PREP:** *20 mins* | **COOK:** *20 mins*

INGREDIENTS

375 g/13 oz (1 rectangular sheet,
35 x 23 cm/14 x 9 inches) ready-
rolled puff pastry
40 g/1½ oz butter
350 g/12 oz baby leeks, thickly
sliced diagonally
1 tbsp chopped fresh oregano
125 g/4½ oz vegetarian goat's
cheese, sliced or crumbled
milk, for brushing
salt and pepper (optional)

1. Preheat the oven to 220°C/425°F/Gas Mark 7. Cut the pastry into six 12-cm/4½-inch squares.

2. Place the pastry squares on a baking sheet and use the tip of a sharp knife to score each square about 1-cm/½-inch from the edge all around.

3. Melt the butter in a frying pan, add the leeks and gently fry, stirring frequently, for 4–5 minutes until soft. Add the oregano, season with salt and pepper, if using, and divide the leek mixture between the pastry squares, placing it inside the scored lines.

4. Top each tartlet with cheese and brush the pastry with milk. Bake in the preheated oven for 12–15 minutes until risen and golden brown. Serve warm.

CRUSTLESS COURGETTE & BROAD BEAN QUICHE

SERVES: *4* | **PREP:** *25 mins, plus chilling* | **COOK:** *1 hour, plus cooling*

INGREDIENTS

135 g/4¾ oz wholemeal spelt flour

70 g/2½ oz baking margarine (from a block), chopped

½ tsp salt

2 tbsp water

250 g/9 oz courgettes, cut into 5-mm/¼-inch thick batons

8 sprays cooking spray, for oiling

100 g/3½ oz broad beans

3 eggs

275 ml/9 fl oz semi-skimmed milk

25 g/1 oz freshly grated Parmesan-style vegetarian cheese

2 tbsp chopped fresh mint

pinch of freshly grated nutmeg

10 g/¼ oz wholemeal spelt flour, for dusting

125 g/4½ oz baby new potatoes, unpeeled, cut into 1-cm/½-inch dice

pepper (optional)

200 g/7 oz mixed salad leaves, to serve

1. Lightly rub together the flour and margarine in a mixing bowl until the mixture resembles fine breadcrumbs. Add the salt and stir, then stir in the water and mix until a ball forms. Wrap the dough in clingfilm and chill in the refrigerator for 30 minutes.

2. Meanwhile, preheat the grill to high. Place the courgettes on a baking sheet and spray with cooking spray to coat, then cook under the preheated grill until slightly charred and soft, turning halfway through. Steam the broad beans until just tender. Combine the eggs, milk, cheese, mint, nutmeg, and pepper to taste, if using, in a bowl.

3. Preheat the oven to 190°C/375°F/Gas Mark 5. Remove the pastry from the refrigerator and roll out on a lightly floured surface into a rough round, then cut out a neat round using a 20-cm/8-inch flan dish as a guide.

4. Line the base of the dish with the pastry round and prick all over. Cover with baking paper and baking beans and bake in the preheated oven for 15 minutes. Remove the paper and beans and return to the oven for a further 5 minutes.

5. Spray the inside edges of the flan dish with cooking spray. Spoon the courgettes, broad beans and potatoes evenly into the dish, then gently pour over the egg mixture. Return to the oven and bake for 25 minutes, or until the filling is set but still with some wobble, and the top is golden.

6. Leave to cool in the dish for 15 minutes. Serve warm or cold with the salad leaves.

EASY RICE & PEAS

SERVES: 4 | **PREP:** 10 mins | **COOK:** 25–30 mins

INGREDIENTS

2 tbsp olive oil

1 onion, sliced

1 garlic clove, crushed

1 tbsp chopped thyme

400 ml/14 fl oz vegetable stock

200 g/7 oz basmati rice

4 tbsp coconut milk

400 g/14 oz canned red kidney
*   beans, drained and rinsed*

salt and pepper (optional)

fresh thyme sprigs, to garnish

1. Heat the oil in a large saucepan, add the onion and fry over a medium heat, stirring, for about 5 minutes until soft.

2. Add the garlic and thyme and stir-fry for 30 seconds. Stir the stock into the pan and bring to the boil.

3. Stir in the rice, then reduce the heat, cover and simmer for 12–15 minutes until the rice is just tender.

4. Stir in the coconut milk and beans, then season to taste with salt and pepper, if using.

5. Cook over a low heat for 2–3 minutes, stirring occasionally, until thoroughly heated. Serve hot, garnished with thyme.

TOFU PARCELS

SERVES: *4* | **PREP:** *15 mins* | **COOK:** *10–15 mins*

INGREDIENTS

2 tbsp olive oil, plus extra for
*   brushing*
1 garlic clove, crushed
250 g/9 oz firm tofu, cut into chunks
250 g/9 oz cherry tomatoes, halved
1 small red onion, thinly sliced
handful of fresh basil leaves
salt and pepper (optional)
crusty bread, to serve

1. Preheat the oven to 220°C/425°F/Gas Mark 7. Brush four
30-cm/12-inch squares of double-thickness foil with the oil. Mix the
remaining oil with the garlic.

2. Divide the tofu, tomatoes, onion and basil between the foil
squares, sprinkle with salt and pepper to taste, if using, and spoon
over the garlic-flavoured oil.

3. Fold over the foil to enclose the filling and seal firmly. Place on a
baking sheet in the preheated oven and cook for 10–15 minutes until
heated through.

4. Carefully open the parcels and serve with crusty bread to mop up
the juices.

GREEN BEAN
PROTEIN BURST

SERVES: *4* | **PREP:** *15 mins* | **COOK:** *15 mins*

INGREDIENTS

400 g/14 oz tofu, drained

2 tbsp soy sauce

2 garlic cloves, crushed

*3 -cm/1¼-inch piece fresh ginger,
    grated*

½ tsp chilli flakes

*200 g/7 oz fresh or frozen broad
    beans, thawed if frozen*

*300 g/10½ oz runner beans,
    trimmed and sliced diagonally*

1 tbsp coconut oil

*1 red pepper, deseeded and
    chopped*

1 tsp garam masala

1 tsp tomato purée

*400 ml/14 fl oz canned coconut
    milk*

*100 g/3½ oz frozen soya beans,
    thawed*

1 tbsp lime juice

2 tbsp salted cashew nuts

fresh coriander, to garnish

1. Cut the tofu into cubes and place in a non-metallic bowl.

2. Mix the soy sauce, garlic, ginger and chilli flakes together and pour over the tofu.

3. Meanwhile, bring a large saucepan of water to the boil, add the broad beans and runner beans and blanch for 4 minutes. Drain.

4. Heat the coconut oil in a wok or large frying pan, add the red pepper and stir-fry for 2–3 minutes.

5. Add the garam masala and tomato purée and cook for 1 minute, then pour in the coconut milk. Bring to the boil, then add the broad beans, runner beans and soya beans and simmer for 4–5 minutes until the beans are tender.

6. Add the tofu and lime juice and cook for a further 2–3 minutes until the tofu is heated through.

7. Serve in four warmed bowls, sprinkled with the cashew nuts and garnished with coriander.

COUSCOUS WITH ROAST
CHERRY TOMATOES & PINE NUTS

SERVES: *4* | **PREP:** *15 mins, plus standing* | **COOK:** *7–8 mins*

INGREDIENTS

300 g/10½ oz cherry tomatoes

3 tbsp olive oil

125 g/4½ oz couscous

200 ml/7 fl oz boiling water

25 g/1 oz pine nuts, toasted

5 tbsp roughly chopped fresh mint

finely grated rind of 1 lemon

½ tbsp lemon juice

salt and pepper (optional)

crisp green salad and vegetarian
  feta cheese, to serve

1. Preheat the oven to 220°C/425°F/Gas Mark 7. Place the tomatoes and 1 tablespoon of the oil in a ovenproof dish. Toss together, then roast for 7–8 minutes in the preheated oven until the tomatoes are soft and the skins have burst. Leave to stand for 5 minutes.

2. Put the couscous in a heatproof bowl. Pour over the boiling water, cover and leave to stand for 8–10 minutes until soft and the liquid has been absorbed.

3. Fluff up the couscous with a fork.

4. Add the tomatoes and their juices, the pine nuts, mint, lemon rind, lemon juice and the remaining oil. Season with salt and pepper, if using, then gently toss together. Serve the couscous warm or cold, with a green salad and some feta cheese.

SOUFFLÉ JACKET POTATOES

SERVES: *4* | **PREP:** *20 mins* | **COOK:** *1 hour 20 mins–1 hour 40 mins*

INGREDIENTS

4 large baking potatoes, about
   400 g/14 oz each
oil, for brushing
2 tbsp milk or single cream
2 eggs, separated
100 g/3½ oz vegetarian Cheddar
   cheese, grated
15 g/½ oz butter
4 spring onions, finely chopped
salt and pepper (optional)

1. Preheat the oven to 200°C/400°F/Gas Mark 6. Place the potatoes on a baking sheet, brush with oil and rub with salt, if using. Bake in the preheated oven for 1–1¼ hours until tender. Do not switch off the oven.

2. Cut a slice from the top of the potatoes and scoop out the flesh, leaving about a 5-mm/¼-inch thick shell. Put the flesh into a bowl. Add the milk, egg yolks and half the cheese and mash together.

3. Melt the butter in a small saucepan, add the spring onions and stir-fry for 1–2 minutes until soft. Reserve a spoonful for the garnish. Stir into the potato mixture and season to taste with salt and pepper, if using.

4. Whisk the egg whites in a clean, grease-free bowl until they hold soft peaks. Lightly fold them into the potato mixture, then spoon the mixture back into the shells.

5. Place the filled potatoes on the baking sheet and sprinkle the remaining cheese on top. Bake for 15–20 minutes until golden. Garnish with the reserved spring onions and serve immediately.

CAULIFLOWER CHEESE

SERVES: *4–6* | **PREP:** *20 mins* | **COOK:** *20 mins*

INGREDIENTS

1 head of cauliflower, trimmed and
cut into florets (675 g/1 lb 8 oz
prepared weight)
40 g/1½ oz butter
40 g/1½ oz plain flour
475 ml/16 fl oz milk
115 g/4 oz vegetarian Cheddar
cheese, finely grated
whole nutmeg, for grating
1 tbsp freshly grated Parmesan-
style vegetarian cheese
salt and pepper (optional)

1. Add a little salt, if using, to a large saucepan of water and bring to the boil. Add the cauliflower, bring back to the boil and cook for 4–5 minutes. It should still be firm. Drain, place in a warmed 1.5-litre/2½-pint gratin dish and keep warm.

2. Melt the butter in the rinsed-out pan over a medium heat and stir in the flour. Cook for 1 minute, stirring constantly.

3. Remove the pan from the heat and gradually stir in the milk until you have a smooth consistency.

4. Return the pan to a low heat and continue to stir while the sauce comes to the boil and thickens. Reduce the heat and simmer gently, stirring constantly, for about 3 minutes until creamy and smooth.

5. Remove from the heat and stir in the Cheddar cheese and a good grating of the nutmeg. Taste and season with salt and pepper, if using. Meanwhile, preheat the grill to high.

6. Pour the hot sauce over the cauliflower, top with the Parmesan-style cheese and place under the grill to brown. Serve immediately.

GRILLED AUBERGINES WITH RED PEPPER, FETA & MINT

SERVES: *4* | **PREP:** *20 mins, plus cooling and standing* | **COOK:** *20 mins*

INGREDIENTS

1 red pepper, halved and deseeded

2 large firm aubergines, sliced crossways into 2-cm/¾-inch slices

olive oil, for brushing

2 garlic cloves, crushed

juice of 1 lemon

1½ tsp cumin seeds, crushed

50 g/1¾ oz vegetarian feta cheese, crumbled

2 tbsp roughly chopped fresh mint leaves

sea salt flakes and pepper (optional)

1. Preheat the grill to high. Put the red pepper halves cut side down in a roasting tray. Place under a very hot grill for about 10 minutes, or until the skin is black and blistered.

2. Place the peppers in a polythene bag and leave for 10 minutes to loosen the skin. Peel off the skin and cut the pepper flesh into 5-mm/¼-inch dice.

3. Preheat a ridged griddle pan over a high heat. Brush the aubergine slices with oil on both sides and place in the pan, in batches, if necessary. Cook for 2 minutes on each side until grill marks appear.

4. Carefully remove the aubergine slices from the pan. Cut the larger slices in half.

5. In a large bowl, combine the garlic, red pepper, lemon juice and cumin. Season to taste with salt and pepper, if using.

6. Add the aubergine slices, turning carefully to coat, then arrange on a serving platter. Scatter over the cheese and mint leaves and serve at room temperature.

MAPLE TOFU WITH
EGG-FRIED RICE

SERVES: *4* | **PREP:** *10 mins* | **COOK:** *20 mins*

INGREDIENTS

1 egg

2 tsp sesame oil

3 tbsp coconut oil

200 g/7 oz long-grain rice, cooked

½ tsp ground turmeric

100 g/3½ oz frozen peas, thawed

4 spring onions, finely chopped

100 g/3½ oz beansprouts

50 g/1¾ oz cashew nuts

340 g/11¾ oz tofu, drained and
*   dried on kitchen paper (drained*
*   weight), cut into chunks*

3 garlic cloves, crushed

3 tbsp soy sauce

2 tbsp maple syrup

1 tbsp rice vinegar

3 pak choi, quartered lengthways

2 tbsp sesame seeds, toasted

1. Beat together the egg and sesame oil and set aside. Heat 2 tablespoons of the coconut oil in a wok or large frying pan, add the rice and turmeric and stir-fry for 3–4 minutes.

2. Add the peas, spring onions, beansprouts and cashew nuts and stir–fry for 3 minutes.

3. Push the rice to one side of the wok, pour in the egg mixture and leave to set for a few seconds, then move it around with chopsticks to break it up. Stir into the rice, then remove from the heat and cover while you cook the tofu.

4. Heat the remaining coconut oil in a frying pan, add the tofu and cook for 4–5 minutes, turning frequently, until light brown all over.

5. Mix the garlic, soy sauce, maple syrup and vinegar together, add to the tofu and cook, stirring occasionally, for 2–3 minutes until the sauce thickens. Meanwhile, steam the pak choi.

6. Divide the rice between four warmed bowls, top with the pak choi and maple tofu, sprinkle with the sesame seeds and serve.

SOBA NOODLES WITH
A HONEY-SOY DRESSING

SERVES: *4* | **PREP:** *10 mins* | **COOK:** *10 mins*

INGREDIENTS

225 g/8 oz dried soba noodles

185 g/6½ oz cabbage, shredded

2 carrots, shredded

*185 g/6½ oz soya beans, shelled
    and blanched*

4 spring onions, thinly sliced

toasted sesame seeds, to garnish

DRESSING

3 tbsp reduced-salt soy sauce

2 tbsp rice wine vinegar

1 tbsp clear honey

1 tsp sesame oil

1. Cook the noodles according to the packet instructions. Drain, rinse well with cold water and set aside to cool completely.

2. Meanwhile, to make the dressing, whisk together the soy sauce, vinegar, honey and oil in a small bowl.

3. Combine the noodles, cabbage, carrots, beans and spring onions in a large bowl and toss to mix. Add the dressing and toss again to combine. Serve immediately, garnished with toasted sesame seeds.

SPICY VEGETABLE
& TOFU UDON NOODLES

SERVES: *4* | **PREP:** *5 mins* | **COOK:** *15 mins*

INGREDIENTS

225 g/8 oz French beans, topped
and tailed and cut into 2.5-cm/
1-inch pieces
2 tbsp water
2 tbsp sriracha
2 tbsp rice vinegar
2 tbsp soy sauce
350 g/12 oz dried udon noodles
1 tbsp vegetable oil
1 tbsp sesame oil
2½ garlic cloves, finely chopped
225 g/8 oz extra firm tofu, cut into
2.5-cm/1-inch cubes
225 g/8 oz baby spinach
toasted sesame seeds, to garnish

1. Place the beans in a microwave-safe bowl with the water. Cover and microwave on high for 2 minutes, then drain.

2. Stir together the sriracha, vinegar and soy sauce in a small bowl.

3. Cook the noodles according to the packet instructions. Drain and set aside.

4. Meanwhile, heat the vegetable oil and sesame oil in a large frying pan over a medium–high heat. Add the garlic and cook, stirring, for 1 minute. Add the tofu and beans and cook, stirring occasionally, for 1 minute until the beans are tender and the tofu is beginning to brown. Stir in the spinach and cook for 2 minutes until it wilts. Add the noodles and sauce mixture and toss to combine well.

5. Serve immediately, garnished with toasted sesame seeds.

UDON NOODLES
WITH KALE & MISO

SERVES: *4* | **PREP:** *10 mins* | **COOK:** *30 mins*

INGREDIENTS

2 tbsp olive oil

*1 large red onion, halved and thinly
    sliced*

½ tsp salt

*1 tbsp Chinese black rice vinegar or
    balsamic vinegar*

350 g/12 oz dried udon noodles

2 garlic cloves, finely chopped

350 g/12 oz kale, shredded

2 tbsp white miso paste

4 tbsp Chinese rice wine or mirin

4 tbsp water

2 tbsp rice vinegar

1 tbsp unsalted butter

*2 tbsp toasted sesame seeds, to
    garnish*

1. Heat 1 tablespoon of the oil in a large frying pan over a medium-high heat. Add the onion and ¼ teaspoon of the salt, reduce the heat to medium-low and cook, stirring occasionally, for 15–20 minutes, until the onion is very soft and beginning to turn golden. Remove from the heat and stir in the black rice vinegar.

2. Meanwhile, cook the noodles according to the packet instructions. Drain and transfer to a large bowl. Keep warm.

3. Transfer the cooked onions to a bowl and keep warm. Add the remaining oil to the pan and heat over a medium–high heat. Add the garlic and cook, stirring, for 1 minute. Add the kale with the remaining salt and cook, stirring frequently, for 4 minutes, until wilted. Remove from the heat and keep warm.

4. Combine the miso paste, wine, water and rice vinegar in a small saucepan and bring to the boil over a medium-high heat, stirring constantly until the miso is fully incorporated. Reduce the heat to medium-low and simmer for 2–3 minutes, until the sauce thickens. Remove from the heat and immediately stir in the butter until it is completely melted. Add the sauce to the noodles and toss well.

5. Serve the noodles in small bowls. Arrange some of the kale in a pile on top, with a pile of the onions alongside. Garnish with the sesame seeds and serve immediately.

PASTA PESTO

INGREDIENTS

450 g/1 lb dried tagliatelle
salt (optional)

PESTO

2 garlic cloves
25 g/1 oz pine nuts
pinch of salt
115 g/4 oz fresh basil leaves, plus
*   extra to garnish*
125 ml/4 fl oz olive oil
55 g/2 oz freshly grated Parmesan-
*   style vegetarian cheese*

1. To make the pesto, put the garlic, pine nuts and salt into a food processor and process briefly. Add the basil and process to a paste.

2. With the motor still running, gradually add the oil. Scrape into a bowl and beat in the cheese. Season to taste with salt.

3. Add a little salt, if using, to a large saucepan of water and bring to the boil. Add the tagliatelle, bring back to the boil and cook for 8–10 minutes until tender but still firm to the bite.

4. Drain well, return to the pan and toss with half the pesto. Divide between warmed serving dishes and top with the remaining pesto. Garnish with basil and serve immediately.

CHILLI BROCCOLI PASTA

INGREDIENTS

225 g/8 oz dried tortiglioni

225 g/8 oz broccoli

50 ml/2 fl oz extra virgin olive oil

2 large garlic cloves, chopped

2 fresh red chillies, deseeded and diced

8 cherry tomatoes, halved if large (optional)

salt (optional)

chopped fresh basil or parsley, to garnish

1. Add a little salt, if using, to a large saucepan of water and bring to the boil. Add the pasta, bring back to the boil and cook for 8–10 minutes until the pasta is tender but still firm to the bite. Remove from the heat, drain, rinse with cold water and drain again. Set aside.

2. Meanwhile, cut the broccoli into florets. Add a little salt, if using, to a separate saucepan of water and bring to the boil, then add the broccoli, bring back to the boil and cook for 5 minutes. Drain, rinse with cold water and drain again.

3. Heat the oil in the pasta pan. Add the garlic, chillies, and tomatoes, if using. Cook over a high heat for 1 minute.

4. Add the broccoli to the pan, mix well and cook for 2 minutes to heat through. Add the pasta, mix well to combine with the other ingredients and cook for a further 1 minute.

5. Remove the pasta from the heat, tip into a large serving bowl and serve immediately, garnished with basil.

FETTUCCINE WITH TOMATO & MUSHROOM SAUCE

SERVES: *4* | **PREP:** *15 mins* | **COOK:** *25–30 mins*

INGREDIENTS

450 g/1 lb dried fettuccine

15 g/½ oz butter

2 tbsp grated Parmesan-style vegetarian cheese

salt (optional)

TOMATO & MUSHROOM SAUCE

25 g/1 oz butter

2 tbsp olive oil

1 large onion, finely chopped

2 garlic cloves, finely chopped

1 celery stick, finely chopped

400 g/14 oz canned chopped tomatoes

2 tbsp tomato purée

4 tbsp vegetarian dry red wine

115 g/4 oz mushrooms, sliced

brown sugar, to taste

1 tbsp chopped fresh basil

salt and pepper (optional)

1. To make the sauce, melt the butter with the oil in a saucepan. Add the onion, garlic and celery and cook over a low heat, stirring occasionally, for 5 minutes until soft. Stir in the tomatoes, tomato purée, wine and mushrooms. Increase the heat to medium and bring to the boil, then reduce the heat and simmer, stirring occasionally, for 15–20 minutes until thickened.

2. Meanwhile, add a little salt, if using, to a large saucepan of water and bring to the boil. Add the pasta, bring back to the boil and cook for 8–10 minutes until tender but still firm to the bite. Drain, tip into a warmed serving dish and toss with the butter.

3. Stir sugar to taste and the basil into the sauce and season to taste with salt and pepper, if using. Pour the sauce over the pasta, toss well and sprinkle with the cheese. Serve immediately.

SPAGHETTI OLIO E AGLIO

SERVES: *4* | **PREP:** *10 mins* | **COOK:** *15 mins*

INGREDIENTS

450 g/1 lb dried spaghetti
125 ml/4 fl oz extra virgin olive oil
3 garlic cloves, finely chopped
3 tbsp chopped fresh flat-leaf
  parsley
salt and pepper (optional)

1. Add a little salt, if using, to a large saucepan of water and bring to the boil. Add the pasta, bring back to the boil and cook for 8–10 minutes until tender but still firm to the bite.

2. Meanwhile, heat the oil in a heavy-based frying pan. Add the garlic and a pinch of salt, if using, and cook over a low heat, stirring constantly, for 3–4 minutes, or until golden. Do not allow the garlic to brown or it will taste bitter. Remove the pan from the heat.

3. Drain the pasta and transfer to a warmed serving dish. Pour in the garlic-flavoured oil, then add the chopped parsley and season to taste with salt and pepper, if using. Toss well and serve immediately.

CHAPTER FOUR

DINNER

WHOLEMEAL LINGUINE
WITH MARINATED TOFU

SERVES: 4 | **PREP:** *15 mins, plus marinating* | **COOK:** *15 mins*

INGREDIENTS

175 g/6 oz tofu, cut into cubes
(drained weight)
350 g/12 oz wholemeal linguine
1 tbsp olive oil, for frying
125 g/4½ oz chestnut mushrooms,
sliced
2 fresh thyme sprigs, leaves only
juice of ½ lemon
salt and pepper (optional)
chopped fresh parsley and freshly
grated Parmesan-style vegetarian
cheese, to garnish

MARINADE

1 tbsp olive oil
juice and zest of ½ lime
1 garlic clove, crushed
¼ tsp chilli flakes
2 tbsp soy sauce
2 tbsp clear honey

1. To make the marinade, mix all the marinade ingredients together in a large bowl. Add the tofu cubes, making sure each piece is coated in the mixture. Leave to marinate for at least 30 minutes.

2. Cook the pasta according to the packet instructions.

3. Meanwhile, heat the oil in a frying pan, add the mushrooms and cook for 5–6 minutes over a medium heat. Toss in the thyme leaves and lemon juice just before removing from the heat.

4. Heat a griddle pan until hot, add the tofu and cook over a medium heat for 5–6 minutes until golden.

5. Drain the pasta and tip it into a large bowl, add the mushroom mixture and tofu and season to taste with salt and pepper, if using. Toss together.

6. Serve the pasta garnished with the chopped parsley and cheese.

QUINOA CHILLI

SERVES: *4* | **PREP:** *15 mins* | **COOK:** *40 mins*

INGREDIENTS

50 g/1¾ oz red quinoa

1 tbsp olive oil

1 onion, diced

2 green chillies, deseeded and diced

1½ tsp smoked paprika

1 tsp chilli powder

2 tsp ground cumin powder

½ tsp cayenne pepper

2 garlic cloves, crushed

*400 g/14 oz canned chopped
    tomatoes*

*400 g/14 oz canned kidney beans,
    drained and rinsed*

*400 g/14 oz canned flageolet beans,
    drained and rinsed*

100 ml/3½ fl oz water

*15 g/½ oz fresh coriander leaves,
    chopped*

*2 tbsp frozen sweetcorn kernels,
    thawed*

soured cream, to serve

1. Cook the quinoa according to the packet instructions.

2. Meanwhile, heat the oil in a large saucepan, add the onion and sauté over a medium heat for 3–4 minutes until soft.

3. Add the chillies to the pan and cook for 1 minute. Stir in the spices and garlic and cook for a further 1 minute.

4. Drain the quinoa and add to the pan along with the tomatoes, beans and water. Bring to a simmer and cook for 30 minutes, stirring occasionally, until thickened. Stir in half the coriander leaves.

5. Divide the chilli between four warmed serving bowls and scatter the sweetcorn kernels and remaining coriander over the top. Serve with soured cream.

LAYERED POTATO &
MUSHROOM PIE

SERVES: *2–4* | **PREP:** *20 mins* | **COOK:** *55 mins*

INGREDIENTS

butter, for greasing
500 g/1 lb 2 oz waxy potatoes,
   thinly sliced and parboiled
150 g/5½ oz mixed mushrooms,
   sliced
1 tbsp chopped fresh rosemary
4 tbsp snipped fresh chives, plus
   extra to garnish
2 garlic cloves, crushed
150 ml/5 fl oz double cream
salt and pepper (optional)

1. Preheat the oven to 190°C/375°F/Gas Mark 5. Grease a large baking dish with butter.

2. Layer a quarter of the potatoes in the base of the dish. Arrange one third of the mushrooms on top of the potatoes and sprinkle with one third of the rosemary, chives and garlic. Continue making the layers in the same order, and finish with a layer of potatoes on top.

3. Pour the double cream evenly over the top of the potatoes. Season to taste with salt and pepper, if using.

4. Bake in the preheated oven for 45 minutes, until golden brown. Garnish with chives and serve immediately.

MACARONI CHEESE

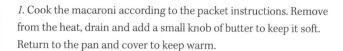

SERVES: *4* | **PREP:** *15–20 mins* | **COOK:** *30–35 mins*

INGREDIENTS

250 g/9 oz dried macaroni

600 ml/1 pint milk

½ tsp grated nutmeg

*55 g/2 oz butter, plus extra for
cooking the pasta*

55 g/2 oz plain flour

*200 g/7 oz mature vegetarian
Cheddar cheese, grated*

*55 g/2 oz freshly grated Parmesan-
style vegetarian cheese*

200 g/7 oz baby spinach

salt and pepper (optional)

1. Cook the macaroni according to the packet instructions. Remove from the heat, drain and add a small knob of butter to keep it soft. Return to the pan and cover to keep warm.

2. Put the milk and nutmeg into a separate saucepan over a low heat and heat until warm, but do not boil. Put the butter into a heavy-based saucepan over a low heat, melt the butter, add the flour and stir to make a roux. Cook gently for 2 minutes. Add the milk a little at a time, whisking it into the roux, then cook for about 10–15 minutes to make a loose, custard-style sauce.

3. Add three quarters of the Cheddar cheese and the Parmesan-style cheese and stir through until they have melted in, then add the spinach, season to taste with salt and pepper, if using, and remove from the heat.

4. Preheat the grill to high. Put the macaroni into a shallow heatproof dish, then pour the sauce over. Scatter the remaining cheese over the top and place the dish under the preheated grill. Grill until the cheese begins to brown, then serve immediately.

WINTER ROOT VEGETABLE TAGINE

SERVES: *4* | **PREP:** *25 mins* | **COOK:** *1 hour*

INGREDIENTS

1 tbsp olive oil

2 red onions, thickly sliced

2 large garlic cloves, crushed

2 tbsp tomato purée

2 tbsp harissa paste

2 carrots, cut into thick batons

100 g/3½ oz potatoes, cut into
*   3-cm/1¼-inch chunks*

200 g/7 oz sweet potatoes, cut into
*   3-cm/1¼-inch chunks*

200 g/7 oz swede, cut into 15 mm/⅝
*   inch thick rounds, then quartered*

600 ml/1 pint reduced-salt
*   vegetable stock*

150 g/5½ oz cooked butter beans or
*   cannellini beans*

300 g/10½ oz canned chopped
*   tomatoes*

200 g/7 oz wholewheat couscous

large handful of fresh flat-leaf
*   parsley, chopped*

salt and pepper (optional)

1. Heat the oil in a flameproof casserole, add the onions and cook over a medium-low heat for 5 minutes, or until soft and transparent. Add the garlic, tomato purée and harissa paste and cook, stirring, for 1 minute.

2. Add the carrots, potatoes, sweet potatoes and swede. Pour in the stock, add pepper, if using, and bring to a simmer. Cover and cook for 30 minutes, or until the vegetables are almost soft, stirring once halfway through.

3. Stir in the beans and tomatoes and cook for a further 15 minutes. Press some of the beans into the side of the casserole dish to break them up and thicken the sauce. Check the seasoning, adding more pepper, if using, and a pinch of salt, if using.

4. Meanwhile, prepare the couscous according to the packet instructions.

5. Scatter the parsley over the tagine and serve immediately with the couscous.

LENTIL BOLOGNESE

SERVES: *4* | **PREP:** *15–20 mins* | **COOK:** *30–40 mins*

INGREDIENTS

175 g/6 oz green lentils
2 tbsp olive oil
1 large onion, chopped
2 garlic cloves, crushed
2 carrots, chopped
2 celery sticks, chopped
800 g/1 lb 12 oz canned chopped
*   tomatoes*
150 ml/5 fl oz vegetable stock
1 red pepper, deseeded and
*   chopped*
2 tbsp tomato purée
2 tsp very finely chopped fresh
*   rosemary*
1 tsp dried oregano
280 g/10 oz dried spaghetti or
*   linguine*
handful of basil leaves, torn
salt and pepper (optional)
freshly grated Parmesan-style
*   vegetarian cheese, to serve*

1. Put the lentils in a saucepan and cover with cold water. Bring to the boil and simmer for 20–30 minutes until just tender. Drain well.

2. Meanwhile, heat the oil in a large saucepan. Add the onion, garlic, carrots and celery. Cover and cook over a low heat for 5 minutes. Stir in the tomatoes, stock, red pepper, tomato purée, rosemary and oregano. Cover and simmer for 20 minutes until the sauce is thickened and the vegetables are tender. Add the lentils and cook, stirring, for a further 5 minutes. Season with salt and pepper, if using.

3. While the sauce is cooking, add a little salt, if using, to a large saucepan of water and bring to the boil. Add the spaghetti, bring back to the boil and cook for 10 minutes, or until tender but still firm to the bite. Drain well, then divide the spaghetti between four warmed bowls. Spoon the sauce over the top and scatter with the basil leaves. Serve immediately with the grated cheese on the side.

BUTTERNUT SQUASH & SPINACH CURRY

SERVES: *4* | **PREP:** *15–20 mins* | **COOK:** *35–40 mins*

INGREDIENTS

1 tbsp groundnut oil

1 large onion, sliced

2 garlic cloves, crushed

3-cm/1¼ -inch piece fresh ginger, finely chopped

75 g/2¾ oz korma curry paste

1 small butternut squash, peeled, deseeded and cut into bite-sized cubes (425 g/15 oz prepared weight)

400 g/14 oz canned chickpeas, drained and rinsed

300 ml /10 fl oz light coconut milk

500 ml /17 fl oz water

½ tsp salt

200 g/7 oz brown basmati rice

200 g/7 oz fresh spinach leaves

large handful of fresh coriander leaves

1. Heat the oil in a large saucepan, then add the onion and cook over a medium-low heat for 5 minutes, or until soft. Add the garlic and ginger and cook, stirring, for 1 minute.

2. Increase the heat to medium-high, add the curry paste and cook for 2 minutes. Add the squash, chickpeas and coconut milk, stir well and bring to a simmer. Reduce the heat to low and simmer for 25 minutes, or until the squash is tender.

3. Meanwhile, put the water into a saucepan with the salt, cover and bring to a simmer. Add the rice and simmer for 25 minutes, or until the rice is tender and the water has been absorbed.

4. Stir the spinach into the curry and leave it to wilt for 1 minute. Scatter the coriander leaves over the curry and serve immediately with the rice.

VEGETARIAN HOT DOGS

SERVES: *4* | **PREP:** *25 mins, plus chilling* | **COOK:** *15 mins*

INGREDIENTS

sunflower oil, for frying
1 small onion, finely chopped
50 g/1¾ oz mushrooms,
   finely chopped
½ red pepper, deseeded and
   finely chopped
400 g/14 oz canned cannellini
   beans, drained and rinsed
100 g/3½ oz fresh breadcrumbs
100 g/3½ oz vegetarian Cheddar
   cheese, grated
1 tsp dried mixed herbs
1 egg yolk
seasoned plain flour

TO SERVE

small bread rolls
fried onion slices
tomato chutney

1. Heat 1 tablespoon of oil in a saucepan. Add the onion, mushrooms and pepper and fry until soft.

2. Mash the cannellini beans in a large bowl. Add the onion, mushroom and pepper mixture, the breadcrumbs, cheese, herbs and egg yolk and mix well. Press the mixture together with your fingers and shape into eight sausages. Roll each sausage in the seasoned flour and chill in the refrigerator for at least 30 minutes.

3. Heat some oil in a frying pan over a medium heat, add the sausages and gently fry for 10 minutes, turning occasionally, until brown all over. Split some bread rolls down the centre and insert a layer of fried onions. Place the sausages in the rolls and serve with tomato chutney.

RICE-CRUSTED VEGETABLE PIE

SERVES: *4* | **PREP:** *20 mins* | **COOK:** *55 mins*

INGREDIENTS

olive oil, for oiling
150 g/5½ oz long-grain brown rice
450 ml/15 fl oz vegetable stock
2 tbsp sesame seeds, toasted
1 egg, beaten
1 red onion, cut into wedges
1 red pepper, deseeded and
  chopped
1 yellow pepper, deseeded and
  chopped
1 courgette, sliced
1 sweet potato, chopped
1 tbsp olive oil
2 tsp cumin seeds
15 g/½ oz fresh basil leaves,
  shredded
2 tbsp walnuts, chopped
2 tbsp flaked almonds
2 tbsp freshly grated Parmesan-
  style vegetarian cheese

1. Preheat the oven to 180°C/350°F/Gas Mark 4. Lightly oil a 23-cm/9-inch pie dish.

2. Cook the rice according to the packet instructions using the stock instead of water.

3. Transfer the cooked rice to a bowl and mix with the sesame seeds and egg.

4. Press the mixture over the base and side of the prepared dish with the back of a spoon. Bake in the preheated oven for 15 minutes.

5. Meanwhile, toss the onion, red pepper, yellow pepper, courgette and sweet potato in a roasting tin with the oil and cumin seeds. Roast in the oven for 30 minutes.

6. Remove the vegetables from the oven and stir through the shredded basil leaves. Spoon into the rice case and return to the oven for 15 minutes.

7. Sprinkle over the walnuts, almonds and grated cheese and cook for a further 10 minutes. Serve hot.

SWEET POTATO & HALLOUMI BURGERS

SERVES: *4–6* | **PREP:** *20 mins, plus chilling* | **COOK:** *40–50 mins*

INGREDIENTS

450 g/1 lb sweet potatoes, cut into
*   chunks*
175 g/6 oz broccoli florets, cut into
*   small pieces*
2–3 garlic cloves, crushed
1 red onion, finely chopped or
*   grated*
1½–2 fresh red jalapeño chillies,
*   deseeded and finely chopped*
175 g/6 oz vegetarian halloumi
*   cheese, grated*
2 tbsp wholemeal flour
2–3 tbsp sunflower oil
450 g/1 lb onions, sliced
1 tbsp chopped fresh coriander
salt and pepper (optional)

1. Add a little salt, if using, to a saucepan of water and bring to the boil. Add the sweet potato and cook for 15–20 minutes, or until tender. Drain and mash. Bring a separate saucepan of water to the boil, add the broccoli and cook for 3 minutes, then drain and plunge into cold water. Drain again, then add to the mashed sweet potato.

2. Stir in the garlic, red onion, chilli, cheese, and salt and pepper to taste, if using. Mix well and shape into four to six equal-sized patties, then coat in the flour. Cover and chill in the refrigerator for at least 1 hour.

3. Heat 1½ tablespoons of the oil in a heavy-based frying pan. Add the onions and fry over a medium heat for 12–15 minutes, or until soft. Stir in the coriander and set aside.

4. Place the burgers in the pan, adding more oil if necessary. Cook over a medium heat for 5–6 minutes on each side, or until they are cooked through.

5. Top the burgers with the fried onions and coriander and serve.

PORTOBELLO MUSHROOM BURGERS WITH MOZZARELLA

SERVES: *4* | **PREP:** *20 mins* | **COOK:** *6–10 mins*

INGREDIENTS

4 tsp olive oil

2 tsp red wine vinegar

1 garlic clove, finely chopped

*4 large Portobello mushrooms, caps
  only*

*4–8 slices fresh vegetarian
  mozzarella cheese*

*4 x 15-cm/6-inch square pieces
  focaccia, split in half*

50 ml/2 fl oz vegetarian pesto

salt and pepper (optional)

*tomato slices and baby rocket
  leaves, to serve*

1. Preheat the oven to 160°C/325°F/Gas Mark 3. Whisk together the oil, vinegar and garlic in a medium-sized bowl. Place the mushrooms gill side up on a baking tray, then drizzle with the vinaigrette and season to taste with salt and pepper, if using.

2. Place under a preheated grill and cook for about 5–8 minutes until the mushrooms are tender. Place the cheese slices on top and cook for a further 1–2 minutes until bubbling. Meanwhile, put the focaccia on a lower rack in the preheated oven for 5 minutes to warm through.

3. Lightly spread the focaccia with the pesto, then add the mushrooms. Top with the tomato slices and rocket and serve immediately.

PARSNIP LAYERED CASSEROLE

INGREDIENTS

3 tbsp olive oil

600 g/1 lb 5 oz parsnips,
  thinly sliced

1 tsp fresh thyme leaves

1 tsp caster sugar

300 ml/10 fl oz double cream

600 g/1 lb 5 oz tomatoes,
  thinly sliced

1 tsp dried oregano

150 g/5½ oz vegetarian Cheddar
  cheese, grated

salt and pepper (optional)

1. Preheat the oven to 180°C/350°F/Gas Mark 4.

2. Heat the oil in a frying pan over a medium heat, add the parsnips, thyme, sugar, and salt and pepper to taste, if using, and cook, stirring frequently, for 6–8 minutes until golden and soft.

3. Spread half the parsnips over the base of a gratin dish. Pour over half the cream, then arrange half the tomatoes in an even layer across the parsnips. Season to taste with salt and pepper, if using, and scatter over half the oregano. Sprinkle over half the cheese. Top with the remaining parsnips and tomatoes. Sprinkle with the remaining oregano, season to taste with salt and pepper, if using, and pour over the remaining cream. Scatter over the remaining cheese.

4. Cover the casserole with foil and bake in the preheated oven for 40 minutes, or until the parsnips are tender. Remove the foil and return to the oven for a further 5–10 minutes until golden and bubbling. Serve immediately.

PENNE IN TOMATO SAUCE
WITH TWO CHEESES

SERVES: *4* | **PREP:** *15 mins* | **COOK:** *30–35 mins*

INGREDIENTS

450 g/1 lb dried penne

115 g/4 oz vegetarian mozzarella cheese, diced

55 g/2 oz freshly grated Parmesan-style vegetarian cheese

TOMATO SAUCE

25 g/1 oz butter

2 tbsp olive oil

2 shallots, finely chopped

2 garlic cloves, finely chopped

1 celery stick, finely chopped

400 g/14 oz canned chopped tomatoes

2 tbsp tomato purée

brown sugar, to taste

1 tsp dried oregano

100 ml/3½ fl oz water

salt and pepper (optional)

1. To make the tomato sauce, melt the butter with the oil in a saucepan. Add the shallots, garlic and celery and cook over a low heat, stirring occasionally, for 5 minutes until soft. Stir in the tomatoes, tomato purée, sugar to taste, oregano and water and season to taste with salt and pepper, if using. Increase the heat to medium and bring to the boil, then reduce the heat and simmer, stirring occasionally, for 15–20 minutes until thickened.

2. Meanwhile, add a little salt, if using, to a large, heavy-based saucepan of water and bring to the boil. Add the penne, bring back to the boil and cook for 8–10 minutes, or until just tender but still firm to the bite. Drain and return to the pan.

3. Add the tomato sauce, mozzarella cheese and Parmesan-style cheese to the pasta and toss well over a very low heat until the cheeses have melted. Transfer to a warmed serving dish and serve.

BUTTERNUT SQUASH BOWL

SERVES: *4* | **PREP:** *10 mins* | **COOK:** *50 mins*

INGREDIENTS

2 butternut squash
2 tbsp olive oil
75 g/2¾ oz brown basmati rice
75 g/2¾ oz wild rice
1 tsp coconut oil
4 spring onions, trimmed and sliced
3-cm/1¼-inch piece fresh ginger,
* grated*
1 lemon grass stalk, trimmed and
* finely sliced*
1 tbsp Thai green curry paste
400 ml/14 fl oz canned coconut
* milk*
400 g/14 oz canned green lentils,
* drained and rinsed*
100 g/3½ oz cavolo nero
1 tbsp golden sesame seeds
1 tbsp black sesame seeds
fresh coriander leaves, to garnish

1. Preheat the oven to 200°C/400°F/Gas Mark 6.

2. Halve the squash, scoop out the seeds and score the flesh with a sharp knife.

3. Place the four squash halves on a baking tray, drizzle with the olive oil and roast in the preheated oven for 40 minutes. Meanwhile, cook the brown rice and wild rice according to the packet instructions.

4. While the rice is cooking, heat the coconut oil in a frying pan. Add the spring onions, ginger and lemon grass and cook for 1 minute, then stir in the curry paste and cook for a further 1 minute.

5. Add the coconut milk and lentils and bring to the boil. Simmer for 15 minutes.

6. Drain the rice and add to the lentil mixture with the cavolo nero. Simmer for 3–4 minutes.

7. Remove the squash from the oven and divide the lentil and rice mixture between the four halves.

8. Sprinkle with the sesame seeds and bake for a further 10 minutes. Garnish with coriander leaves and serve.

BAKED AUBERGINE WITH TOMATO SAUCE

SERVES: 4 | **PREP:** 25–30 mins | **COOK:** 55–60 mins

INGREDIENTS

40 g/1½ oz butter, plus extra for
*   greasing*
40 g/1½ oz dry breadcrumbs
1 large aubergine, cut into 1-cm/
*   ½-inch slices*
1 tsp dried oregano
55 g/2 oz Parmesan-style
*   vegetarian cheese, grated*
salt (optional)

TOMATO SAUCE

25 g/1 oz butter
2 tbsp olive oil
1 small onion, finely chopped
1 garlic clove, finely chopped
1 celery stick, finely chopped
400 g/14 oz canned chopped
*   tomatoes*
2 tbsp tomato purée
brown sugar, to taste
1 tbsp chopped fresh basil, plus
*   extra to garnish*
1 tsp dried oregano
100 ml/3½ fl oz water
salt and pepper (optional)

1. To make the sauce, melt the butter with the oil in a saucepan. Add the onion, garlic and celery and cook over a low heat, stirring occasionally, for 5 minutes until soft. Stir in the tomatoes, tomato purée, sugar to taste, basil, oregano and water and season to taste with salt and pepper, if using. Increase the heat to medium and bring to the boil, then reduce the heat and simmer, stirring occasionally, for 15–20 minutes until thickened.

2. Preheat the oven to 230°C/450°F/Gas Mark 8. Grease a baking sheet with butter. Melt the butter and pour it into a shallow dish. Spread out the breadcrumbs in a separate shallow dish. Dip the aubergine slices first in the melted butter and then in the breadcrumbs to coat. Put them on the prepared baking sheet and season to taste with salt, if using. Bake in the preheated oven for 20 minutes until golden brown and tender.

3. Remove the baking sheet from the oven. Top each aubergine slice with a spoonful of tomato sauce and sprinkle with a little of the oregano and cheese. Return to the oven and bake for a further 10 minutes until the topping is golden brown. Transfer to a serving dish, garnish with basil and serve immediately.

ROAST CAULIFLOWER, KALE & CHICKPEA BOWL

SERVES: *4* | **PREP:** *20 mins* | **COOK:** *40 mins*

INGREDIENTS

1 tsp ground turmeric

1 tsp mustard seeds

½ tsp cumin seeds

½ tsp ground ginger

½ tsp ground coriander

½ tsp ground cinnamon

1 head of cauliflower, broken
  into florets

400 g/14 oz canned chickpeas,
  drained and rinsed

2 red onions, thickly sliced

2 tbsp olive oil

200 g/7 oz kale, shredded

200 g/7 oz fresh wholemeal
  breadcrumbs

3 tbsp walnuts, chopped

2 tbsp flaked almonds

55 g/2 oz freshly grated Parmesan-
  style vegetarian cheese

1. Preheat the oven to 200°C/400°F/Gas Mark 6.

2. Dry-fry the turmeric, mustard seeds, cumin seeds, ginger, coriander and cinnamon in a small frying pan for 2 minutes, or until the mustard seeds start to 'pop'.

3. Place the cauliflower florets, chickpeas and onion slices in a large roasting tin. Sprinkle with the spices and toss well together.

4. Drizzle over the oil and toss again. Roast in the preheated oven for 20 minutes.

5. Stir the kale into the roast vegetables, and roast for a further 10 minutes, until the vegetables are tender and slightly charred.

6. Mix the breadcrumbs, walnuts, almonds and cheese together and sprinkle over the vegetables. Roast for a further 5–8 minutes until golden. Divide between four warmed bowls and serve immediately.

MUSHROOM &
WALNUT OPEN TART

SERVES: *4* | **PREP:** *20 mins* | **COOK:** *30–40 mins*

INGREDIENTS

1 tbsp olive oil

15 g/½ oz butter

1 red onion, sliced

1 garlic clove, crushed

*500 g/1 lb 2 oz closed-cup chestnut
    mushrooms, sliced*

85 g/3 oz walnuts, chopped

*2 tbsp chopped fresh flat-leaf
    parsley, plus extra to garnish*

*500 g/1 lb 2 oz ready-made
    shortcrust pastry*

plain flour, for dusting

beaten egg, for glazing

salt and pepper (optional)

1. Preheat the oven to 200°C/400°F/Gas Mark 6. Heat the oil and butter in a large frying pan, add the onion and stir-fry for 2–3 minutes until soft but not brown.

2. Add the garlic and mushrooms and cook, stirring, for 3–4 minutes until soft. Cook until any liquid has evaporated, then remove from the heat and stir in the walnuts, parsley, and salt and pepper to taste, if using.

3. Roll out the pastry on a lightly floured work surface to a 35-cm/ 14-inch round and place on a large baking sheet. Pile the mushroom mixture onto the pastry, leaving a 9-cm/3½-inch border.

4. Lift the edges of the pastry and tuck up around the filling, leaving an open centre. Brush the pastry with beaten egg to glaze.

5. Bake in the preheated oven for 25–30 minutes until the pastry is golden brown. Serve warm, sprinkled with parsley.

CARROT
TARTE TATIN

SERVES: *4* | **PREP:** *20 mins* | **COOK:** *45–50 mins*

INGREDIENTS

*600 g/1 lb 5 oz young carrots, cut
    into 2.5-cm/1-inch chunks*

2 tbsp clear honey

25 g/1 oz butter

1 small bunch fresh thyme, chopped

*350 g/12 oz ready-made puff pastry,
    thawed if frozen*

plain flour, for dusting

salt and pepper (optional)

1. Add a little salt to a large saucepan of water and bring to the boil. Add the carrots, bring back to the boil and cook for 10–15 minutes until just tender. Drain, toss with the honey, butter and thyme and season to taste with salt and pepper, if using.

2. Preheat the oven to 200°C/400°F/Gas Mark 6. Spoon the carrots over the base of a 20-cm/8-inch tarte tatin tin or round cake tin with a depth of about 3 cm/1¼ inches. Roast in the preheated oven for 15 minutes, or until the carrots are caramelized. Remove from the oven but do not switch off the oven.

3. Roll out the pastry on a floured work surface into a round large enough to fit the tin and give a 2-cm/¾-inch overlap. Lay the pastry carefully over the carrots and tuck the edges down between the carrots and the side of the tin to make a border. Bake in the oven for 15 minutes, or until the pastry is puffed and golden.

4. Remove the tart from the oven and invert the tin onto a plate to release. Cut the tart into slices and serve immediately.

MIXED NUT ROAST WITH CRANBERRY & RED WINE SAUCE

SERVES: *4* | **PREP:** *20 mins* | **COOK:** *35 mins*

INGREDIENTS

2 tbsp butter, plus extra for greasing
2 garlic cloves, chopped
1 large onion, chopped
50 g/1¾ oz pine nuts, toasted
75 g/2¾ oz hazelnuts, toasted
50 g/1¾ oz ground walnuts
50 g/1¾ oz ground cashew nuts
100 g/3½ oz wholemeal
  breadcrumbs
1 egg, lightly beaten
2 tbsp chopped fresh thyme
275 ml/9 fl oz vegetable stock
salt and pepper (optional)
sprigs of fresh thyme, to garnish

CRANBERRY & RED WINE SAUCE

175 g/6 oz fresh cranberries
100 g/3½ oz caster sugar
300 ml/10 fl oz vegetarian red wine
1 cinnamon stick

1. Preheat the oven to 180°C/350°F/Gas Mark 4. Grease a 450-g/1-lb loaf tin and line it with greaseproof paper.

2. Melt the butter in a saucepan over a medium heat. Add the garlic and onion and cook, stirring, for about 3 minutes. Remove the pan from the heat.

3. Grind the pine nuts and hazelnuts in a mortar with a pestle. Stir into the pan with the walnuts and cashew nuts and add the breadcrumbs, egg, thyme, stock and seasoning.

4. Spoon the mixture into the loaf tin and level the surface. Cook in the centre of the preheated oven for 30 minutes or until cooked through and golden and a skewer inserted into the centre of the loaf comes out clean.

5. Halfway through the cooking time, make the sauce. Put all the ingredients into a saucepan and bring to the boil. Reduce the heat and simmer, stirring occasionally, for 15 minutes.

6. Remove the nut roast from the oven and turn out onto a serving platter. Garnish the roast with sprigs of thyme and serve with the cranberry and red wine sauce.

PUMPKIN & CHESTNUT RISOTTO

SERVES: *4* | **PREP:** *20 mins* | **COOK:** *35–40 mins*

INGREDIENTS

1 tbsp olive oil

40 g/1½ oz butter

1 small onion, finely chopped

225 g/8 oz pumpkin, diced

225 g/8 oz chestnuts, cooked and shelled

280 g/10 oz risotto rice

150 ml/5 fl oz vegetarian dry white wine

1 tsp crumbled saffron threads (optional), dissolved in 4 tbsp of the stock

1 litre/1¾ pints simmering vegetable stock

85 g/3 oz freshly grated Parmesan-style vegetarian cheese, plus extra for serving

salt and pepper (optional)

1. Heat the oil with 25 g/1 oz of the butter in a deep saucepan over a medium heat until the butter has melted. Stir in the onion and pumpkin and cook, stirring occasionally, for 5 minutes, or until the onion is soft and starting to turn golden and the pumpkin is beginning to colour.

2. Roughly chop the chestnuts and add to the mixture. Stir thoroughly to coat.

3. Reduce the heat, add the rice and mix to coat in oil and butter. Cook, stirring constantly, for 2–3 minutes, or until the grains are translucent. Add the wine and cook, stirring constantly, for 1 minute until it has reduced.

4. Add the saffron liquid to the rice, if using, and cook, stirring constantly, until the liquid has been absorbed.

5. Gradually add the simmering stock, a ladleful at a time, stirring constantly. Add more liquid as the rice absorbs each addition. Increase the heat to medium so that the liquid bubbles. Cook for 20 minutes, or until all the liquid has been absorbed and the rice is creamy. Season to taste with salt and pepper, if using.

6. Remove from the heat and add the remaining butter and the cheese, stirring until melted. Sprinkle with cheese and serve.

WILD MUSHROOM RISOTTO

SERVES: *6* | **PREP:** *20 mins, plus soaking* | **COOK:** *30–35 mins*

INGREDIENTS

55 g/2 oz dried ceps or morel
  mushrooms
about 500 g/1 lb 2 oz mixed
  fresh wild mushrooms, such
  as ceps, field mushrooms and
  chanterelles, halved if large
4 tbsp olive oil
3–4 garlic cloves, finely chopped
55 g/2 oz butter
1 onion, finely chopped
350 g/12 oz risotto rice
60 ml/2 fl oz dry white vermouth
1.2 litres/2 pints simmering
  vegetable stock
115 g/4 oz freshly grated Parmesan-
  style vegetarian cheese
4 tbsp chopped fresh flat-leaf
  parsley
salt and pepper (optional)

1. Place the dried mushrooms in a heatproof bowl and add boiling water to cover. Set aside to soak for 30 minutes, then carefully lift out and pat dry. Strain the soaking liquid through a sieve lined with kitchen paper and reserve.

2. Trim the fresh mushrooms and gently brush clean. Heat 3 tablespoons of the oil in a large frying pan. Add the fresh mushrooms and stir-fry for 1–2 minutes. Add the garlic and the soaked mushrooms and cook, stirring frequently, for 2 minutes. Transfer to a plate.

3. Heat the remaining oil and half the butter in a large heavy-based saucepan. Add the onion and cook over a medium heat, stirring occasionally, for 2 minutes until soft. Reduce the heat, stir in the rice and cook, stirring constantly, for 2–3 minutes, until translucent. Add the vermouth and cook, stirring, for 1 minute until reduced.

4. Gradually add the hot stock, a ladleful at a time, until all the liquid is absorbed and the rice is creamy. Add half the reserved mushroom soaking liquid to the risotto and stir in the mushrooms. Season to taste with salt and pepper, if using, and add more mushroom liquid, if necessary. Remove the pan from the heat, stir in the remaining butter, grated cheese and chopped parsley and serve.

CHAPTER FIVE

BAKING & DESSERTS

ROASTED FRUIT CRUMBLE

SERVES: *4* | **PREP:** *15 mins* | **COOK:** *35–40 mins*

INGREDIENTS

4 apricots, stoned and quartered

1 tbsp caster sugar

200 g/7 oz raspberries

200 g/7 oz blackberries

55 g/2 oz rolled oats

40 g/1½ oz wholemeal flour

25 g/1 oz pecan nuts

10 g/¼ oz sesame seeds

60 g/2¼ oz muscovado sugar

60 g/2¼ oz coconut oil

1. Preheat the oven to 180°C/350°F/Gas Mark 4.

2. Place the apricot quarters in a roasting tin, sprinkle with the sugar and roast in the preheated oven for 15 minutes.

3. Spoon the apricots into four ovenproof dishes and sprinkle over the remaining fruit.

4. Place the remaining ingredients in a food processor and process until they resemble very lumpy breadcrumbs.

5. Spoon the crumble over the fruit, place the dishes on a baking sheet and bake in the oven for 20–25 minutes until the tops are golden and the fruit is bubbling.

FRUIT COCKTAIL
POPS

SERVES: *8* | **PREP:** *35 mins, plus cooling & freezing* | **COOK:** *6–8 mins*

INGREDIENTS

225 g/8 oz strawberries, hulled

2 small ripe peaches, peeled, stoned and roughly chopped (or 250 g/ 9 oz canned peaches, drained)

4 large kiwi fruits, peeled and roughly chopped

SUGAR SYRUP

2 tbsp caster sugar

5 tbsp water

YOU WILL ALSO NEED

8 x 125-ml/4-fl oz ice lolly moulds

8 ice lolly sticks

1. To make the sugar syrup, put the sugar and water into a saucepan over a low heat and stir until the sugar has dissolved. Increase the heat, bring to the boil, then reduce the heat again and simmer for 3–4 minutes. Remove from the heat and leave to cool completely before using.

2. Put the strawberries in a blender and whizz until puréed. Stir in 2 tablespoons of the sugar syrup. Pour the mixture into eight 125-ml/ 4-fl oz ice pop moulds. Freeze for 2 hours or until firm.

3. When the strawberry mixture is frozen, put the peaches in the blender and whizz until puréed. Stir in half the remaining sugar syrup. Pour the peach mixture over the frozen strawberry mixture. Insert the ice pop sticks and freeze for 2 hours, or until firm.

4. When the peach mixture is frozen, put the kiwi fruits in the blender and whizz until puréed. Stir in the remaining sugar syrup. Pour the kiwi mixture over the frozen peach mixture and freeze for 2 hours, or until firm.

5. To unmould the ice pops, dip the moulds into warm water for a few seconds and gently release the pops while holding the sticks.

RICH CHOCOLATE TARTS

SERVES: *8* | **PREP:** *35–40 mins, plus chilling & cooling* | **COOK:** *25–30 mins*

INGREDIENTS

225 g/8 oz plain flour, plus extra
for dusting
115 g/4 oz butter, diced
2 tbsp icing sugar
1 egg yolk
2–3 tbsp cold water

FILLING

250 g/9 oz plain chocolate, broken
into pieces, plus extra to decorate
115 g/4 oz butter
50 g/1¾ oz icing sugar
300 ml/10 fl oz double cream

1. Place the flour in a large bowl. Add the butter and rub it in with your fingertips until the mixture resembles breadcrumbs. Add the icing sugar, egg yolk and enough water to form a soft dough. Cover and chill for 15 minutes. Turn out onto a lightly floured work surface, roll out and use to line eight 10-cm/4-inch shallow tart tins. Chill in the refrigerator for 30 minutes.

2. Preheat the oven to 200°C/400°F/Gas Mark 6. Prick the base of each tartlet case with a fork and line with a little crumpled foil. Bake in the preheated oven for 10 minutes, then remove the foil and bake for a further 5–10 minutes until crisp. Transfer to a wire rack to cool. Reduce the oven temperature to 160°C/325°F/Gas Mark 3.

3. To make the filling, place the chocolate, butter and icing sugar in a heatproof bowl set over a saucepan of gently simmering water and heat until melted. Remove from the heat and stir in 200 ml/7 fl oz of the cream. Remove the tartlet cases from the tins and place on a baking sheet. Fill each case with the chocolate mixture. Bake for 5 minutes. Leave to cool completely, then chill until required. To serve, whip the remaining cream and pipe or spoon into the centre of each tart. Grate some plain chocolate and sprinkle over the tarts.

CAPPUCCINO SOUFFLÉS

SERVES: *6* | **PREP:** *30 mins, plus cooling* | **COOK:** *25 mins*

INGREDIENTS

butter, for greasing

2 tbsp whipping cream

2 tsp instant espresso coffee granules

2 tbsp coffee-flavoured liqueur

3 large eggs, separated, plus 1 extra egg white

2 tbsp golden caster sugar, plus extra for coating

150 g/5½ oz plain chocolate, melted and cooled

cocoa powder, for dusting

1. Preheat the oven to 190°C/375°F/Gas Mark 5. Lightly grease six 175-ml/6-fl oz ramekins and coat the insides with caster sugar.

2. Place the cream in a small, heavy-based saucepan and heat gently. Stir in the coffee until it has dissolved, then stir in the liqueur. Divide the coffee mixture between the prepared ramekins.

3. Place the egg whites in a clean bowl and whisk until soft peaks hold, then gradually whisk in the sugar until stiff but not dry. Stir the egg yolks and melted chocolate together in a separate bowl, then stir in a little of the whisked egg whites. Gradually fold in the remaining egg whites.

4. Divide the mixture between the ramekins, then place them on a baking sheet and bake in the preheated oven for 15 minutes, or until just set. Dust with sifted cocoa powder and serve immediately.

PEACH COBBLER

SERVES: *4–6* | **PREP:** *20–30 mins* | **COOK:** *35 mins*

INGREDIENTS

FILLING

6 peaches, peeled and sliced

4 tbsp caster sugar

½ tbsp lemon juice

1½ tsp cornflour

½ tsp almond or vanilla extract

vanilla or pecan ice cream, to serve

TOPPING

185 g/6½ oz plain flour

115 g/4 oz caster sugar

1½ tsp baking powder

½ tsp salt

85 g/3 oz butter, diced

1 egg

6 tbsp milk

1. Preheat the oven to 220°C/425°F/Gas Mark 7. Place the peaches in a 23-cm/9-inch square baking dish. Add the sugar, lemon juice, cornflour and almond extract and toss together. Bake in the preheated oven for 20 minutes.

2. Meanwhile, to make the topping, sift the flour, all but 2 tablespoons of the sugar, the baking powder and the salt into a bowl. Rub in the butter with your fingertips until the mixture resembles breadcrumbs. Mix the egg and 5 tablespoons of the milk in a jug, then mix into the dry ingredients with a fork until a soft, sticky dough forms. If the dough seems too dry, stir in the extra tablespoon of milk.

3. Reduce the oven temperature to 200°C/400°F/Gas Mark 6. Remove the peaches from the oven and drop spoonfuls of the topping over the surface, without smoothing. Sprinkle with the remaining sugar, return to the oven and bake for a further 15 minutes, or until the topping is golden brown and firm – the topping will spread as it cooks. Serve hot or at room temperature, with ice cream.

WHOLEGRAIN DARK CHOCOLATE BROWNIES

MAKES: *20 brownies* | **PREP:** *20 mins* | **COOK:** *25 mins, plus cooling*

INGREDIENTS

175 g/6 oz dates, stoned and chopped

125 ml/4 fl oz water

100 g/3½ oz plain chocolate, at least 70% cocoa solids, broken into pieces

70 g/2½ oz unsalted butter

55 g/2 oz light muscovado sugar

25 g/1 oz cocoa powder

25 g/1 oz plain wholemeal flour

1 tsp baking powder

2 eggs, beaten

1. Preheat the oven to 180°C/350°F/Gas Mark 4. Line a 20-cm/8-inch shallow square non-stick cake tin with baking paper, snipping it into the corners diagonally then pressing into the tin so that both the base and sides are lined.

2. Put the dates and water in a saucepan. Bring the water to the boil, cover, reduce the heat to medium–low and simmer for 5 minutes, or until the dates are soft. Add the chocolate, butter and sugar and stir until melted. Remove from the heat.

3. Sift the cocoa into a bowl, then mix in the flour and baking powder. Add the eggs and the flour mixture to the pan and stir until smooth. Pour into the prepared tin and spread in an even layer. Bake in the preheated oven for 18–20 minutes, or until well risen and the centre is only just set.

4. Leave to cool in the tin for 15 minutes. Lift the cake out of the tin, cut into 20 brownies and peel off the paper.

KEY LIME PIE

SERVES: *8* | **PREP:** *25–30 mins, plus cooling & chilling* | **COOK:** *25 mins*

INGREDIENTS

BASE

175 g/6 oz digestive biscuits or
*   ginger biscuits*
2 tbsp caster sugar
½ tsp ground cinnamon
70 g/2½ oz butter, melted, plus
*   extra for greasing*

FILLING

400 ml/14 fl oz canned condensed
*   milk*
125 ml/4 fl oz freshly squeezed lime
*   juice*
finely grated rind of 3 limes
4 egg yolks
whipped cream, to serve

1. Preheat the oven to 160°C/325°F/Gas Mark 3. Grease a 23-cm/9-inch round tart tin, about 4 cm/1½ inches deep.

2. To make the base, put the biscuits, sugar and cinnamon in a food processor and process until fine crumbs form – do not process to a powder. Add the melted butter and process again until moist.

3. Tip the mixture into the prepared tin, pressing evenly into the base and sides. Place on a baking sheet and bake in the preheated oven for 5 minutes. Meanwhile, beat the condensed milk, lime juice, lime rind and egg yolks together in a bowl until well blended.

4. Remove the tin from the oven, pour the filling into the base and spread out to the edges. Return to the oven for a further 15 minutes, or until the filling is set around the edges but still wobbly in the centre. Leave to cool completely on a wire rack, then cover and chill in the refrigerator for at least 2 hours. Serve spread thickly with whipped cream.

STRAWBERRY CHEESECAKE

SERVES: *8* | **PREP:** *25 mins, plus cooling* | **COOK:** *1 hour 10 mins, plus cooling*

INGREDIENTS

BASE

55 g/2 oz unsalted butter
200 g/7 oz digestive biscuits,
  crushed
85 g/3 oz chopped walnuts

FILLING

450 g/1 lb vegetarian mascarpone
  cheese
2 eggs, beaten
3 tbsp caster sugar
250 g/9 oz white chocolate, broken
  into pieces
300 g/10½ oz strawberries, hulled
  and quartered

TOPPING

175 g/6 oz vegetarian mascarpone
  cheese
50 g/1¾ oz white chocolate
  shavings
4 strawberries, halved

1. Preheat the oven to 150°C/300°F/Gas Mark 2. Melt the butter in a saucepan over a low heat and stir in the biscuits and walnuts.

2. Spoon into a 23-cm/9-inch round springform cake tin and press evenly over the base with the back of a spoon. Set aside.

3. To make the filling, beat the mascarpone cheese in a bowl until smooth, then beat in the eggs and sugar.

4. Place the chocolate in a heatproof bowl set over a saucepan of gently simmering water and heat until melted. Remove from the heat and leave to cool slightly, then stir into the cheese mixture. Stir in the strawberries.

5. Spoon the mixture into the tin, spreading evenly and smoothing the surface. Bake in the preheated oven for 1 hour, or until just firm.

6. Switch off the oven and leave the cheesecake inside with the door slightly ajar until completely cold. Transfer to a serving plate.

7. Spread the mascarpone cheese on top, decorate with the chocolate shavings and the strawberry halves and serve.

RASPBERRY, CHIA SEED & PECAN POTS

SERVES: *4* | **PREP:** *10 mins* | **COOK:** *No cooking*

INGREDIENTS

400 g/14 oz raspberries

2 tbsp chia seeds

1 mango, stoned, peeled and chopped

400 g/14 oz Greek-style natural yogurt

3 kiwi fruits, peeled and sliced

chopped toasted pecan nuts, to decorate

1. Place the raspberries in a food processor and blitz until smooth, then place in a bowl. Stir in the chia seeds and leave to stand – they will gradually thicken the mixture to a jam-like consistency.

2. Place the mango into the rinsed out food processor and whizz until smooth. Lightly stir through the yogurt, leaving trails of mango showing.

3. Layer the yogurt, raspberry-chia mixture and kiwi slices in four glasses, finishing with yogurt on top.

4. Sprinkle with chopped pecan nuts to serve.

RASPBERRY & WHITE CHOCOLATE BRÛLÉES

SERVES: 6 | **PREP:** 20 mins, plus cooling & chilling | **COOK:** 10 mins

INGREDIENTS

200 g/7 oz white chocolate, broken
    into pieces
200 ml/7 fl oz single cream
500 g/1 lb 2 oz Greek-style natural
    yogurt
225 g/8 oz raspberries
75 g/2¾ oz granulated sugar
3 tbsp water

1. Place the chocolate and cream in a heatproof bowl set over a saucepan of gently simmering water and heat, stirring occasionally, until the chocolate has melted. Remove from the heat and leave to cool slightly.

2. Stir the chocolate mixture into the yogurt, then fold in the raspberries. Divide between six 150-ml/5-fl oz ramekins and level the surfaces with the back of a teaspoon. Chill in the refrigerator for at least 30 minutes.

3. Place the granulated sugar and water in a small, heavy-based saucepan. Heat gently until the sugar dissolves, then increase the heat and boil rapidly for about 4 minutes, without stirring, until the sugar turns a rich caramel colour.

4. Remove from the heat and allow the bubbles to subside, then quickly spoon some caramel over the top of each ramekin. The topping will set almost instantly. Serve immediately or chill and serve within 3 hours while the caramel is still crisp.

CRÈME BRÛLÉE

SERVES: *6* | **PREP:** *20–25 mins, plus chilling* | **COOK:** *2–4 mins*

INGREDIENTS

225–300 g/8–10½ oz mixed soft
fruits, such as blueberries and
stoned fresh cherries
1½–2 tbsp orange liqueur or orange
flower water
250 g/9 oz vegetarian mascarpone
cheese
200 ml/7 fl oz crème fraîche
2–3 tbsp dark muscovado sugar

1. Divide the fruit between six 150-ml/5-fl oz ramekins. Sprinkle with the liqueur.

2. Cream the mascarpone cheese in a bowl until soft, then gradually beat in the crème fraîche.

3. Spoon the cheese mixture over the fruit, smoothing the surface and levelling the tops. Chill in the refrigerator for at least 2 hours.

4. Sprinkle the tops with the sugar. Using a chef's blow torch, grill the tops until caramelized (about 2–3 minutes). Alternatively, cook under a preheated grill, turning the ramekins, for 3–4 minutes, or until the tops are lightly caramelized all over.

5. Serve immediately or chill in the refrigerator for 15–20 minutes before serving.

PINEAPPLE POWER
CHEESECAKE BOWL

SERVES: *4* | **PREP:** *15 mins, plus chilling* | **COOK:** *2 mins*

INGREDIENTS

200 g/7 oz tofu
200 g/7 oz vegetarian cream cheese
2 tbsp maple syrup
grated rind of 1 orange
2 tbsp pecan nuts
400 g/14 oz fresh pineapple, peeled,
  cored and chopped
2 tbsp desiccated coconut flakes
2 tsp clear honey
8 sweet oat cakes

1. Place the tofu, cream cheese and maple syrup in a food processor and process until smooth.

2. Stir in the orange rind and divide the mixture between four small bowls. Chill in the refrigerator for 10 minutes.

3. Dry-fry the pecan nuts, then roughly chop.

4. Divide the pineapple between the bowls, then sprinkle with the chopped nuts and coconut.

5. Drizzle each bowl with a little honey.

6. Serve each portion with two sweet oat cakes.

BLACK RICE PUDDING
WITH GINGER & PINEAPPLE

SERVES: *4* | **PREP:** *10 mins* | **COOK:** *25 mins*

INGREDIENTS

175 g/6 oz black rice

100 ml/3½ fl oz soya single cream

225 g/8 oz fresh pineapple, halved

6 knobs stem ginger, diced

4 tbsp stem ginger syrup

15 g/½ oz fresh mint leaves,
*   shredded*

4 tbsp coconut yogurt

1. Cook the rice according to the packet instructions.

2. Drain the rice and place three quarters of it in a food processor with the soya cream and half the pineapple. Whizz until you have the consistency of rice pudding.

3. Spoon the rice mixture into four glasses.

4. Dice the remaining pineapple and place in a bowl with the diced ginger, syrup and mint. Mix well.

5. Spoon the coconut yogurt over the rice mixture, then pour over the ginger and pineapple mixture to serve.

CHOCOLATE MOUSSE

SERVES: *4–6* | **PREP:** *35 mins, plus cooling & chilling* | **COOK:** *5 mins*

INGREDIENTS

225 g/8 oz plain chocolate, chopped
2 tbsp brandy or triple sec
4 tbsp water
25 g/1 oz unsalted butter, diced
3 large eggs, separated
¼ tsp cream of tartar
55 g/2 oz sugar
125 ml/4 fl oz double cream

1. Please note that infants, the elderly, pregnant women, convalescents and anyone suffering from an illness should avoid eating raw eggs.

2. Place the chocolate, brandy and water in a small saucepan over a low heat and heat, stirring, until smooth. Remove the pan from the heat and beat in the butter. Beat the egg yolks into the chocolate mixture, one at a time, until blended, then leave to cool slightly.

3. Meanwhile, using a hand-held electric mixer, beat the egg whites in a spotlessly clean bowl on low speed until frothy, then gradually increase the speed and beat until soft peaks hold. Sprinkle the cream of tartar over the surface, then add the sugar, a tablespoon at a time, and continue beating until the mixture holds stiff peaks. Beat several tablespoons of the mixture into the chocolate mixture to loosen.

4. In a separate bowl, whip the cream until it holds soft peaks. Spoon the cream over the chocolate mixture, then spoon the remaining white over the cream. Use a large spoon or spatula to fold the chocolate into the cream and egg white. Either spoon the chocolate mousse into a large serving bowl or divide between individual bowls. Cover the bowls with clingfilm and chill in the refrigerator for at least 3 hours before serving.

ICE-CREAM
BROWNIE SUNDAE

SERVES: 6 | **PREP:** 30 mins, plus cooling | **COOK:** 45–50 mins

INGREDIENTS

175 g/6 oz plain chocolate, broken
   into pieces
175 g/6 oz butter, plus extra for
   greasing
175 g/6 oz soft light brown sugar
3 eggs, beaten
115 g/4 oz self-raising flour

CHOCOLATE FUDGE SAUCE

55 g/2 oz plain chocolate, broken
   into pieces
55 g/2 oz soft light brown sugar
55 g/2 oz unsalted butter
3 tbsp milk

TO SERVE

6 large scoops vanilla ice cream
1 tbsp pecan nuts, chopped
6 fresh cherries or maraschino
   cherries

1. Preheat the oven to 180°C/350°F/Gas Mark 4. Grease a 20-cm/ 8-inch square cake tin and line with baking paper.

2. To make the brownies, place the chocolate and butter in a large heatproof bowl set over a saucepan of gently simmering water and heat until melted. Leave to cool for 5 minutes, then whisk in the sugar and eggs. Sift in the flour and fold in. Pour the mixture into the prepared tin and bake in the preheated oven for 35–40 minutes, or until risen and just firm to the touch. Leave to cool in the tin for 15 minutes, then turn out onto a wire rack and leave to cool completely.

3. To make the sauce, place all the ingredients in a saucepan and heat over a low heat, stirring constantly, until melted. Bring to the boil and bubble for 1 minute. Remove from the heat and leave to stand for 20 minutes.

4. To serve, cut the brownies into six pieces. Place each piece on a serving plate and top with a large scoop of ice cream. Spoon over the warm sauce and decorate with the chopped nuts and cherries.

COURGETTE LOAF CAKE WITH CREAM CHEESE FROSTING

SERVES: *10* | **PREP:** *25 mins* | **COOK:** *1 hour*

INGREDIENTS

175 g/6 oz ground almonds
½ tsp baking powder
½ tsp bicarbonate of soda
3 tbsp stevia
40 g/1½ oz chopped mixed nuts
50 g/1¾ oz butter
2 large eggs, beaten
1 tsp vanilla extract
200 g/7 oz courgettes, coarsely
  grated

FROSTING

200 g/7 oz full-fat vegetarian cream
  cheese
1 tbsp stevia
finely grated zest and juice of
  ¼ unwaxed lemon

1. Preheat the oven to 160°C/325°F/Gas Mark 3. Line a non-stick loaf tin with baking paper.

2. Put the ground almonds, baking powder, bicarbonate of soda, stevia and half the nuts in a large bowl and stir well.

3. Melt the butter in a small saucepan over a medium–low heat. Pour it onto the dry ingredients. Add the eggs, vanilla extract and courgettes and mix well.

4. Spoon the mixture into the prepared tin, spreading in an even layer. Bake in the preheated oven for 55–60 minutes, or until well risen and a skewer inserted into the centre of the cake comes out clean. Leave to cool in the tin for 15 minutes, then turn out, peel off the baking paper and transfer to a wire rack to cool completely.

5. To make the frosting, put the cream cheese and stevia in a large bowl and whisk until light and airy. Add the lemon zest and juice, and whisk again briefly. Using a spatula, spread the frosting over the top of the cake. Decorate with the remaining nuts and serve.

CHOCOLATE & BRAZIL NUT BARS

MAKES: *9 bars* | **PREP:** *20 mins, plus chilling* | **COOK:** *5 mins*

INGREDIENTS

100 g/3½ oz flaked almonds

125 g/4½ oz Brazil nuts,
roughly chopped

70 g/2½ oz unsalted butter

70 g/2½ oz almond butter

1 tsp vanilla extract

50 g/1¾ oz ground almonds

30 g/1 oz desiccated coconut

1½ tbsp rice malt syrup

2 tsp cocoa powder

20 g/¾ oz plain chocolate, 85%
cocoa solids, cut into small
chunks

sea salt (optional)

1. Line a 19-cm/7½-inch square cake tin with baking paper. Toast the flaked almonds and Brazil nuts in a dry frying pan over a high heat until they are light brown, then tip them into a large mixing bowl.

2. Put the unsalted butter and almond butter in a small saucepan and heat over a low heat until melted. Stir in the vanilla extract and a pinch of salt, if using.

3. Add all the remaining ingredients to the toasted nuts, then stir. Add the melted butter mixture and stir again. Tip the mixture into the prepared tin and, using the back of a spoon, spread it out into the corners. Cover and chill in the refrigerator for 30 minutes until set.

4. Cut into nine bars and wrap each one in baking paper. Store in an airtight container in the refrigerator for up to 2 days.

PEANUT BUTTER
& BANANA MUFFINS

MAKES: *12 muffins* | **PREP:** *15 mins* | **COOK:** *15–20 mins*

INGREDIENTS

200 g/7 oz self-raising flour
50 g/1¾ oz buckwheat flour
75 g/2¾ oz golden caster sugar
25 g/1 oz rolled oats
2 bananas, peeled and mashed
100 g/3½ oz crunchy peanut butter
2 eggs, beaten
25 g/1 oz coconut oil, melted
125 ml/4 fl oz milk

1. Preheat the oven to 200°C/400°F/Gas Mark 6. Line a 12-hole muffin tin with paper cases and set aside.

2. Sift the self-raising flour, buckwheat flour and sugar into a large bowl, then mix in the oats.

3. In a separate bowl, mix the mashed banana and peanut butter with the eggs, coconut oil and milk.

4. Stir the banana mixture into the flour mixture, taking care not to over-mix. It's fine if a little flour is still showing when you put them in the oven.

5. Spoon the batter into the paper cases and bake in the preheated oven for 15–18 minutes until risen and golden.

CHOCOLATE & ALMOND BISCOTTI

MAKES: *22 biscotti* | **PREP:** *15 mins* | **COOK:** *50–60 mins, plus cooling*

INGREDIENTS

1 tsp baking powder

150 g/5½ oz plain flour, plus extra for dusting

90 g/3¼ oz buckwheat flour

150 g/5½ oz golden caster sugar

20 g/¾ oz cacao powder

¼ tsp ground cinnamon

4 eggs, beaten

175 g/6 oz blanched almonds, toasted and roughly chopped

100 g/3½ oz plain chocolate, to decorate

100 g/3½ oz white chocolate, to decorate

1. Preheat the oven to 150°C/300°F/Gas Mark 2. Line a baking sheet with non-stick baking paper.

2. Place the baking powder, plain flour, buckwheat flour, sugar, cacao powder and cinnamon in a large bowl and stir together.

3. Add the eggs and stir into the dry ingredients, then add the almonds once the dough starts to come together.

4. Turn out the dough onto a floured work surface and roll it into a long sausage shape, about 35 cm/14 inches long and 6–7 cm/2½–2¾ inches wide. Place on the prepared baking sheet and bake in the preheated oven for 30–40 minutes.

5. Remove the sheet from the oven and leave to cool on a wire rack for 10 minutes.

6. Cut the dough into 1-cm/½-inch thick slices and bake for a further 8–10 minutes on each side until firm. Transfer to a wire rack and leave to cool.

7. Put the plain chocolate and white chocolate into separate heatproof bowls set over saucepans of gently simmering water and heat until melted. Drizzle lines of chocolate over the biscotti to decorate. Leave to set, then serve.

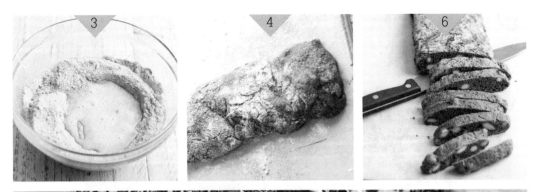

CELEBRATION CHOCOLATE CAKE

SERVES: 8 | **PREP:** *40 mins* | **COOK:** *1 hour 20 mins, plus cooling*

INGREDIENTS

unsalted butter, for greasing
2 raw beetroot (about 200 g/7 oz),
cut into cubes
150 g/5½ oz plain chocolate, at
least 70% cocoa solids, broken
into pieces
25 g/1 oz cocoa powder
2 tsp baking powder
115 g/4 oz plain wholemeal flour
55 g/2 oz brown rice flour
200 g/7 oz unsalted butter, softened
and diced
215 g/7½ oz light muscovado sugar
4 eggs
2 tbsp milk
300 ml/10 fl oz double cream

1. Preheat the oven to 160°C/325°F/Gas Mark 3. Lightly grease and base-line a 20-cm/8-inch round non-stick springform cake tin.

2. Steam the beetroot for 15 minutes, or until tender. Place in a food processor with 4 tablespoons of water from the base of the steamer. Purée until smooth, then leave to cool.

3. Put 115 g/4 oz of the chocolate in a heatproof bowl set over a saucepan of gently simmering water and heat until melted. Sift the cocoa into a separate bowl, then stir in the baking powder, wholemeal flour and rice flour.

4. Cream together the butter and 200 g/7 oz of the sugar in a large bowl. Beat in the eggs, one at a time, alternating with the flour mixture and beating well after each addition. Stir in any remaining flour mixture, the beetroot and chocolate, and beat until smooth, then mix in enough milk to make a soft dropping consistency.

5. Spoon into the prepared tin and spread in an even layer. Bake in the preheated oven for 1 hour until well risen, slightly cracked on top and a skewer inserted into the centre comes out clean. Leave to cool for 15 minutes, then remove from the tin, peel off the paper and transfer the cake to a wire rack.

6. Melt the remaining chocolate in a heatproof bowl set over a saucepan of gently simmering water. Whisk the cream with the remaining sugar. Cut the cake in half and put the bottom half on a serving plate. Spoon one third of the cream onto the base of the cake, add the top half, then spoon the remaining cream on the top. Drizzle with the melted chocolate. Cut into eight wedges to serve.

INDEX

.... ✄ ....

This edition published by Parragon Books Ltd in 2017
LOVE FOOD is an imprint of Parragon Books Ltd

Parragon Books Ltd
Chartist House
15–17 Trim Street
Bath BA1 1HA, UK
www.parragon.com/lovefood

ISBN 978-1-4748-6893-8

Printed in China

Edited by Fiona Biggs
Cover photography by Al Richardson

The cover shot shows the Flatbread Pizza with Garlic
Courgette Ribbons on page 82.

.... *Notes for the Reader* ....

This book uses both metric and imperial measurements.
Follow the same units of measurement throughout;
do not mix metric and imperial. All spoon measurements
are level: teaspoons are assumed to be 5 ml, and tablespoons
are assumed to be 15 ml. Unless otherwise stated, milk
is assumed to be full fat, eggs and individual fruits and
vegetables are medium, pepper is freshly ground black
pepper and salt is table salt. Unless otherwise stated,
all root vegetables should be peeled prior to using.

The times given are an approximate guide only.
Preparation times differ according to the techniques used
by different people and the cooking times may also vary
from those given.

Vegetarians should be aware that some of the ready-made
ingredients used in the recipes in this book might contain
animal products. Always check the packaging before use.